MW01224470

WILDERNESS SON
A LIFETIME OF EXPERIENCES

Floyd Kielczewski

To Tom Klein

by Marlette Kielczewski
as told to her by Floyd Kielczewski

Copyright 2013 Marlette Kielczewski
ALL RIGHTS RESERVED

ISBN-10: 1490564462
ISBN-13: 9781490564463

Library of Congress Control Number: 2013911929
CreateSpace Independent Publishing Platform
North Charleston, South Carolina

Dedication

This book is dedicated to
my father and mother who lived it.

Forward

I grew up with my father's stories. These were tales of incredible adventures as a result of his life in the unsettled wilderness of Northern Ontario. They were all the more real to me as I have some very clear memories of living on the trap line and traveling by snowmobile through the woods in the winter and by boat down the rivers and lakes in the summers before we moved to the United States. Following that move, my father regaled hundreds of people who came to Summer Camp each summer (a.k.a. Summer Education Program or Youth Opportunities United) with these stories over the 35 years he was there. When he finally retired and started spending some part of the winter months in Arizona, I asked him to tell me these stories again in great detail so that we could capture them for posterity. Then, we brought these stories to life by adding old family photos, which transformed them from tall tales to real life adventures.

This is his story.

Acknowledgements

I would like to thank five individuals who generously donated their talent, knowledge, experience, ability, and time to make this a better book.

I wish to thank Kate McKenna for getting me started in the right direction, for her wise counsel and encouragement, and for the initial editing of the book. I would also like to thank Leon Ritchie for taking the time to meticulously retouch and restore some of our old family photos. A good picture truly is worth a thousand words. Dennis Mathewson was born and raised in the same area in Northern Ontario and shared similar experiences. His first-hand knowledge of people, places, and events provided additional detail, clarity and story enrichment. My cousin, Grant Kielczewski, (William John Kielczewski's son) is a Manager of Communications who also possesses a BA in Communications and an MBA in Business Management. Grant generously agreed to lend both his familial understanding and his technical skill to the final editing of the manuscript. This unique combination of perspective and skill was exactly what was required to make the book ready for publication. Finally, I would like to thank Lance Raber for sharing with me his knowledge and experience in the realm of self-publishing. It made this endeavor much less daunting and ensured a quality end product.

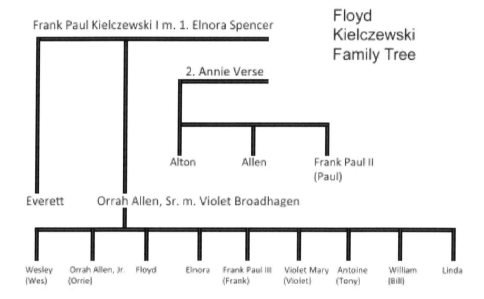

Floyd
Kielczewski
Family Tree

Frank Paul Kielczewski I m. 1. Elnora Spencer

2. Annie Verse

Alton   Allen   Frank Paul II
                                (Paul)

Everett   Orrah Allen, Sr. m. Violet Broadhagen

Wesley   Orrah Allen, Jr.   Floyd   Elnora   Frank Paul III   Violet Mary   Antoine   William   Linda
(Wes)   (Orrie)   (Frank)   (Violet)   (Tony)   (Bill)

Table of Contents

In the Beginning

I was born on December 10, 1932, in the McKenzie Point cabin on Stokes Bay, which is on the northeast end of Rainy Lake in Ontario, Canada. At the time of my birth, this area was considered an unorganized township of Rainy River District, and it is recorded as such on my birth record.

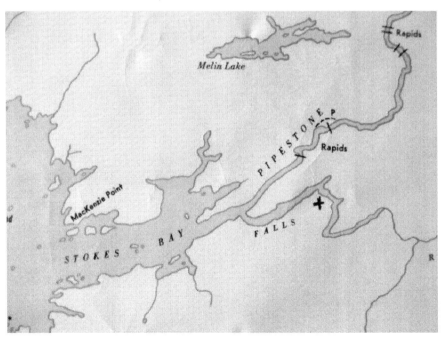

Map of the location of Floyd's birthplace on Rainy Lake as well as an "X" marking the location of the Falls River homestead.

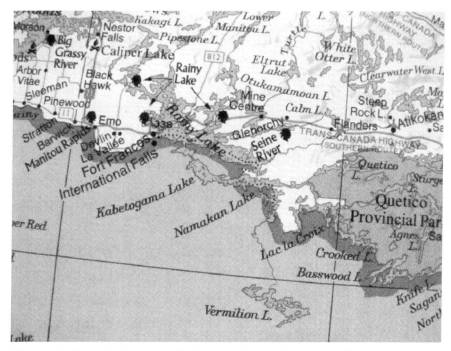

Map of the Canadian/American border including the Rainy Lake District.

Current day photo of McKenzie Point on Rainy Lake.

My father, Orrah Allen Kielczewski, was born in Bryant, Wisconsin, on July 15, 1900. He had an older brother named Everett. When my father was six years old, his mother, who was in her early twenties, died in childbirth delivering a girl, who also died. The baby was named Elnora after her mother. My grandfather, Frank Paul Kielczewski I, had married Elnora Spencer. My grandfather had to leave his two boys with their maternal grandparents, the Spencers, so that he could go and make a living. At the time he was a US Marshal. Eventually he moved to Minnesota, where he worked building the steel bridges, which replaced the old wooden ones.

It was a hard life for the boys, who were not treated well by their grandparents.

Eventually they ran away from their grandparents' farm. Orrah was twelve years old at the time. Orrah and Everett jumped a railroad car that took them to Montana. They ended up working on a cattle ranch not far off the railroad line.

When World War I broke out, Everett decided to join the army. My Dad was not quite old enough to join, and as a result, he ended up jumping another boxcar going north into Canada. He went as far up as Hudson Bay. He went up and down the Nelson River with the Indians from that area. He spent ten years with them and learned many skills, including how to live off the land, how to pole upriver, and how to run white water. Eventually he ended up in Manitoba. It was in Manitoba that he met my mother, Violet Matilda Broadhagen.

My mother was born in Stratford, Ontario, Canada, on July 9, 1911. She spent several years there before she, her parents, and siblings moved up to an area called Goose Lake, near Setting Lake and Wabowden, Manitoba.

In 1928, they settled on Goose Lake because they could not find enough land for homesteading near Setting Lake. It was here that she met my dad. Her pony's feet were stuck in the mud, and my dad came to her aid, freeing the pony.

My dad asked Mr. Broadhagen for my mother's hand in marriage, but her father said no. So they eloped. Of course, her father was angry and wanted the Mounties to go after them, but the Mounties were reluctant to. My mom and dad were married at Cross Lake, Manitoba. She was seventeen, and my dad was twenty-seven. Mother never saw her mother again. Her mother died before I was born.

My parents arrived at my grandfather's camp on the Rat River in the spring of 1929. It had been nearly fifteen years since my dad had seen his father, Frank Kielczewski. During those years, Frank had remarried and had three more sons; Alton, Allen, and Frank Paul II (Paul). My dad worked at the Rat River camp for a while.

My grandfather was a commercial fisherman then. Later on, my uncles Allen and Alton commercially fished those same grounds. In his later years, uncle Allen gave the camp to his son, Terry Kielczewski. Terry worked it for a while but eventually sold it back to the Canadian government.

My father provided for the family by working as a trapper and by guiding deer and moose hunters up at Kielczewski's Camp.

In September of 1929, my parents decided to build their own place on McKenzie Point. It was a humble log cabin, but it was their own. I don't think my mother had anticipated the hardships she would endure and the level of perseverance she would need in her new life. It was a blessing that she could not see what the future would hold.

We lived off the land. We grew it, hunted it, or made it ourselves. What little money we could make from picking logs or trapping was used to purchase staples like flour, wheat, and sugar. Picking logs meant collecting floating logs, which have slipped loose from boom timbers, with a pick.

My mother even made soap from lye. All of her nine children, except the first one, were born at home with my father assisting with their deliveries.

It was on October 31, 1929, that my oldest brother, Wesley Spencer Kielczewski, was born. My dad took my mother to a nursing home in Fort Frances, which was about sixty miles away. My mother told us that he was born breach. She stayed in the nursing home ten days after he was born.

Wes always helped at home. As he grew up, he became good with an axe, trapping, and building boats. Eventually he went to work at a logging camp for John Stewart. John liked Wes and the work he did. Wes went with mom to pick blueberries, and as Orrah Jr. and I got older, we went picking as well. Wes continued to help mother his entire life.

A little over a year later, on December 18, 1930, my mother delivered another boy, named Orrah Allen Kielczewski Jr. He was premature, and mother said she was sure he was not going to live. Orrah did not walk until he was three years old. Now with two small boys, my mother still had to work hard, washing all of the family's clothes by hand, trying to provide meals with meager food supplies, and helping my father with outdoor work.

I was born on a cold day, the tenth of December 1932, at the McKenzie Point Cabin on Stokes Bay, at 3:00 a.m. This cabin, which had been built by my father and mother, was made of rough-hewn white poplar trees. Mud and moss were used to pack the spaces between the logs of this humble home. My father had shot a moose early that day, and he wanted to skin it and cut it up. Although my mother was in the early stages of labor, she managed to help with the moose. A few hours later, she delivered me with my father's assistance. I was their third son.

1934 – Wes, Orrah Jr., and Floyd in front of the McKenzie Point Cabin.

In 1933, the Canadian Mounted Police came through the area and recorded the individuals who were living in the unorganized district. The Kielczewski family was put on the records, and years later it proved to be the only legal record of my birth, citizenship, or documentation substantiating my origin.

Orrah and Violet and their young family made three moves over the next several years. In 1934, they left the McKenzie Point homestead and moved us to Halverson's Camp, which was three miles from the Falls River on Stokes Bay. As was common in those days, the lumber camp was full of lice. So my mother had to burn the mattresses and make all new ones out of deer hair. All of us children had to have our hair cut off. Mother used kerosene to clean everything else, which killed all of the lice. Eventually we did get rid of them. I remember living at Halverson's for five years.

During that time, on April 28, 1934, my sister, the first girl, was born. They named her Elnora after dad's mother and Margaret after my maternal grandmother, who had passed away just before I was born.

An event that clearly stands out in my mind was the forest fire of 1936. I was almost four years old in that hot and dry summer when the fire broke out near McKenzie Point. It was probably due to heat-related thunder and lightning combined with a lack of rain. It was such a big fire that our family had to evacuate the McKenzie Point homestead and move out to Oak Island in Stokes Bay, taking as many supplies with us as time permitted.

We set up a tent on the island in which to live. The rest of the supplies, guns, traps, and equipment were removed and put on a small island south of McKenzie Point in Finland Bay. It was such a ravaging fire that it was discussed for many years after. The fire raged for several days, and burning leaves carried by the wind would land on the tent we were staying in and on the ground around us. We used wet gunnysacks and lake water to put out the sparks. Finally, rain put out the forest fire. We returned to the homestead on McKenzie Point, where our house remained unharmed.

Just two weeks after the forest fires, on September 9, 1936, my brother Frank Paul III (Frank) was born. He was a big baby, weighing about nine pounds, with very fair skin. The cord was wrapped around his neck, and his head was veiled meaning that remnants of the amniotic sac were covering his head immediately after birth.

Orrah Sr. had to run for his pocketknife to cut the veil and unwind the cord so that the baby could get oxygen. My mother would later remark that Frank was a beautiful baby.

In the spring of 1938, we moved to the Kettle River place. It was an old deserted camp where railroad ties had been manufactured. My grandfather, Frank Paul Kielczewski I, was the original owner and operator of the camp. At that time, the camp had been deserted for about twenty years. The main building, which was still standing, was L-shaped and had a kitchen, living room, and two bedrooms. At one point, someone had actually tried to burn the building down. I still remember the burnt ceiling and ridge poles. We picked blueberries, sold them for ten cents a quart, and used the money to purchase paint to make the main building livable.

On July 9, 1938, another girl was born. It was also my mother's twenty-seventh birthday, so the girl was named after her. Violet Mary Kielczewski was the sixth child of Orrah and Violet Kielczewski.

While mother was pregnant with her seventh child, she was hauling wood with a rope over her shoulder, pulling a heavy sleigh. Orrah Sr. was not home as he had taken the dog team and gone trapping on his trap line near the old logging camps. She came into the house and started to hemorrhage. She lay down, elevated the lower half of her body, and packed herself with ice. Orrah Jr. got firewood, stoked up the fires, baked a batch of baking powder biscuits, and cooked something for dinner. He fed the younger children and my mother. The next morning, mother was terribly weak from the loss of blood, so Orrah Jr. stoked up the fires and ran the nine miles down to the old logging camps to get our dad. Although dad made it back very quickly, by the time he returned, mother had stopped hemorrhaging.

On January 6, 1942, my brother, Antoine David, was born. We called him Tony. Tony was born with yellow jaundice. This was due to the fact that food was scarce, and all mother had to eat while she was pregnant with Tony was fried salt pork and onions with potatoes.

We moved to the Falls River in 1947, where we homesteaded, clearing better than an acre of land, including all the stumps. We stayed at this location until 1956, when the family moved to British Columbia.

Falls River homestead in 1954. Due to high water that year, the steamboat is sunk.

Current day photo of the former location of the Falls River homestead.

When I was six years old I would go blueberry picking off Oak Island with mother, Wes, and Orrah Jr. Those were long days in which we picked blueberries all day until there were none left to pick. We sold the blueberries for ten cents a quart, which provided some income. In addition to the hard work of picking blueberries, mother took care of all of us children and the new babies.

One day when we were picking blueberries, I heard something humming in the ground. So I stuck my ear down there, and hornets came out and stung me all over my ear. I ran away screaming. My mother came to my rescue, but I learned a valuable lesson.

When I was seven years old, my dad gave me my first gun, which was an old Mossberg bolt action .22. However, this gun didn't work quite right. So dad made a lever action single-shot from two guns for me. He used the sights and barrel from the Mossberg and the lever action and stock from an old .32 action Stevens, making a .22. I used this gun for years until I bought a new .22 Mossberg bolt action out of Winnipeg.

1943 – Floyd is cleaning his single shot Mossberg bolt action while his dad is making a paddle in front of a tent they had set up so they could trap along the Pipestone River.

School was never an option for my brothers and me. We were expected to join our father to secure a living for the family. I began working at the age of nine, rowing a boat and collecting logs on Rainy Lake. We collected logs that had slipped loose from the boom timbers belonging to the J. A. Mathieu Logging Company.

Our father and we Kielczewski boys collected the logs and towed them to J. A. Mathieu's mill in Fort Frances, Ontario. In 1945, the mill paid us seventy-five cents a log for each log returned. In the four years prior to that, the mill paid fifty cents for each log. The days were long, and it was hard work. The entire summer was spent rowing and retrieving logs. I longed for sleep and did not look forward to daylight. I was constantly worried about losing a log, storms, and high winds. I was never so happy to get out of that business as I was after the last tow down in 1945.

Once summer passed and winter set in, trapping and hunting became our life. My brothers, Wes, Orrah Jr., and I spent the winters with our father, learning the art of trapping and hunting. I was eleven years old when I started trapping with my dad. Wes was fourteen, and Orrah Jr. was thirteen. Ammunition was scarce, so we learned how to make each shot count. I attribute this experience to me becoming an expert marksman and a skilled hunter early in my teenage years.

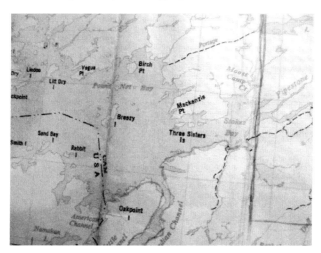

Map of the area in which the Falls River homestead was located. The line to the right is the western edge of the Kielczewski trap line.

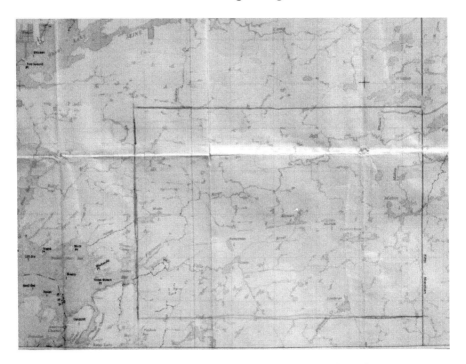

Squared off area on the map indicates the Kielczewski trap line boundaries.

Current day photo of the Falls River.

Current day photo of the Pipestone River.

As spring approached and the rivers opened, my father taught me the art of running rapids. In the spring, when the snow melts, the rivers are higher and the water runs faster and more furiously for about a month. I started running rapids at eleven. This talent would serve me well, as only a few short years later, this unique ability contributed to my success as a guide on Namakan Lake.

Dad helped me build a flat-bottomed skiff when I was twelve. It was made of two and a half inch-thick white pine boards. The skiff was twelve inches deep and thirty-six inches wide, pointed at both ends like a canoe. The bottom had a keel down the center. If I hit a rock or stepped on it wrong, it would spring a leak. To reinforce the bottom of the skiff, we put two keels on each side of the main keel called "sister keels." These keels were made of one-inch-by-one inch Spruce, Jack Pine, or Ash without knots. If a piece of wood with a knot were used, the keel would break where the knot was located. This resolved the issue. However, if it were left out of the water, it would dry out and leak. The solution was to keep it wet. When the lumber was wet, it swelled up and as a result did not leak. This is the boat that I initially used to run rapids. Because the sides were straight and not rounded, I had to be careful when running white water so that it wouldn't flip over. I had that boat for three years.

My dad, brothers, and I worked hard and, in 1942, we purchased a twenty-six-foot wooden steamboat that needed repair. We referred to it as "The Tub." It was purchased from Eddie George of Fort Frances. We thought it had a leak in the steam boiler, so we mixed cornstarch and wheat together and used this mixture to fill in the crack. That would hold for a while, but eventually it would leak again. I began to run the steamboat and could read steam before I could tell time. I remember coming to the Five-Mile Bridge by Fort Frances and knowing to blow the whistle three times. When the bridge controller answered with one long and one short whistle, I knew the train would stop, the bridge would rise, and we would be able to pass through. If the bridge controller answered with three long whistles, I knew that the train was too close to stop, and I would have to wait.

In 1950, we purchased another steamboat, named the *Clipper.* I began to run the steamboat. It was forty-seven feet long with a ten-foot beam, round bottomed, and it went fifteen or sixteen knots, which is about seventeen or eighteen miles per hour.

"The Clipper" steamboat, which was rebuilt by the Kielczewskis.

13

Wes, Orrah Jr., and I became expert canoeists. Dad had taught us to "read white water." When I was twelve, I started running the rapids on the Pipestone River solo and enjoyed the challenge. When I was thirteen, my brother, Frank, who was nine, started going with me. Frank and I were very close as brothers and friends.

In the mid-1950s, I started guiding fishermen out of Namakan Narrows Lodge. I ran Hay and Lady Rapids on Namakan River, first by canoe, and later using a fifteen-foot Larson boat with a twenty-five-horsepower Johnson motor.

I began my hunting career when I was nine by shooting a partridge with my single-shot .22 rifle. I then went on to add rabbits and porcupines.

My mother taught me how to tan deer hides. I practiced the process, and many years later at the summer camp in Orr, Minnesota, I tanned deer hides for a friend of mine. His wife sewed the hides together for him, making a pant and shirt outfit complete with fringe.

My mother also made feather robes. She made an outer cover out of canvas, which could be removed and washed. The robe itself had a flannel cover. She sewed individual pockets, filled them with duck and goose feathers, and then covered the pockets with flannel, which she tied together with yarn every twelve inches. She used store cord to knot it. If the store cord started to break, then she used seaman's twine. She ordered the flannel from Eaton's catalogue. We could sleep in sixty-below weather in these feather robes. Mother made twelve of them so that each of us had one of our own. In addition, she made pillows out of rough grouse feathers.

One year my dad caught a female timber wolf in a trap. When he found her, he knocked her on the nose, rendering the wolf unconscious. He brought the wolf home and called her Gray Girl. He put her on a chain and led her around day after day. Then he put her in harness with the other dogs, and she pulled the sleigh as part of the dog team. He had her for about a year, and then one day he must have had the choke collar on too tight, and she died. My mother never did like the wolf and wasn't a bit sorry when she was gone.

1935 - Orrah Sr. with Gray Girl.

1936 – Orrah Sr. with Gray Girl.

The Old 30-40 Craig—1920s

Dad borrowed his dad's big bear trap, which was worth about five hundred dollars. He went to set the trap, and it had a big ring on it. So he bent the knots on the toggle down and slipped the ring over it. But a bear chewed the knots off and got the trap free. The bear was dragging the trap on his foot, so dad started to chase the bear. He had a well-worn Craig rifle that only had three shots in it because the magazine was bent from an overload of powder. So all he could get in it was three shots. He was gaining on the bear, and all of a sudden that ring snapped over a jack pine knot. When it snapped over the jack pine knot, the bear knew he was cornered, so he wheeled around and charged dad. But my dad was fast, so he shot three times, with all three shots hitting him in the heart. The bear dropped only five feet from him. He said the blood was squirting out and nearly hitting him. That was back in the late twenties, before I was born.

My dad said, "Bears don't usually charge you unless they are cornered." I have the picture of that bear and my dad; with the chain that dad used to drag it out of the woods still around its neck. Later on, dad slipped on wet moss at the edge of a steep bank on the Pipestone River and fell down about twenty feet into the river with his packsack, which included the three-shot Craig. Dad lost the packsack and the gun, which is still at the bottom of the Pipestone River, at the bottom of a rapid in about twenty feet of water.

1920s – Orrah Sr., a bear and the 30-40 Craig his used to shoot it. Orrah hauled the bear out of the woods using the chain pictured around his neck.

Living Off the Land

Dad took an old Stevenson lever action .32 and an aged Mossberg bolt action single-shot with no safety and fixed up the barrel of the Mossberg .22 bolt action. He took the two guns and made them into a .22 single-lever action with an extractor for the rim fire to pull out the empties. I used it for years. I shot beaver and bears with it.

I was nine when I shot my first bird, a rough grouse. It was right above my head, and it was getting dark. About all I could see was the neck, so I took aim and hit him in the neck, cutting his head off. After that I started shooting rabbits and more grouse. We lived off the game we took. It was a matter of survival.

1955 – Floyd on the Big Marsh on the Pipestone River with blue gill ducks he had shot.

When I didn't have a gun, I killed spruce hens with a stone. Spruce hens are pretty tame, and they don't fly.

One time, Frank and I were up on an island on Lindgren Lake building a cabin. Lindgren Lake flows into Bull Moose Lake, and Bull Moose flows into Captain Tom's Lake, which flows into Little Eva Lake, which flows into Namakan Lake.

The faceplate of the German-made sixteen-gauge shotgun I had for shooting game fell off the gun. I didn't realize that I had lost it until I was going to shoot a bird. Since the firing pin goes through the faceplate, I couldn't fire the gun. We were running out of food, so I used a stone to kill a partridge. We prayed to God, asking for help in finding the faceplate because we couldn't use the gun without it.

The next day, we went back to Little Long Lake, southwest of Lindgren Lake and Bull Moose Lake, and found the faceplate in the leaves on the ground.

When we lived in remote wilderness areas, going to a store was something we did only once or twice a year. As a result, all of the meat we ate was from hunting. We lived off the land in the truest sense of the phrase. My mother's garden helped out. She also made feather robes out of duck feathers; tanned buckskin out of deer hides for outerwear and moccasins, and canned meat.

In 1943, my mother shot a thousand squirrels in one month between the end of October and the end of November. She got forty-five squirrels from a box of fifty .22 short shells, so she was a very good shot. She got thirty-five cents a squirrel. The shells were twenty cents a box. She skinned and stretched the hides herself. The money helped us buy items we couldn't make, grow or hunt ourselves.

Mom grew a garden and canned all the vegetables she could. She canned Swiss chard, beans, tomatoes, spinach, pumpkin, squash, and carrots. She made pickles out of cucumbers and canned them. What blueberries my mother didn't sell, she canned.

At the end of every October, we would haul up to five hundred pounds of potatoes from Fort Frances by steamboat. We kept the potatoes, along with carrots, rutabagas, acorn and Hubbard squash from the garden, buried in sand in the root cellar. Because it stayed at forty-five degrees, the vegetables would still be good through the middle of the winter. Also, every year, we hauled up five hundred pounds of whole wheat from Fort Frances, which we ground ourselves. We kept the coarsely ground wheat to make porridge for dog food. In addition to the porridge, we smoked and dried beaver meat for the dogs in our homemade smokehouse. We would take beaver we had caught in traps, debone and de-fat the meat, and then smoke it for three days to dry it out.

In addition to canning vegetables, we canned meat. We routinely canned 150 quarts of venison and 250 quarts of beaver meat to eat. We only canned fresh beaver that we had recently shot or that had drowned within the past twelve hours. We did not can or eat any beaver that had been dead longer due to the possibility of tainting.

There was a law in Canada that you couldn't keep venison past March, even canned venison. The government figured that you were shooting deer and canning it out of season. The rural citizens of Canada raised such a ruckus that they changed the law. In any case, the Mounties wouldn't have known when it was canned because we just backdated the labels.

We killed approximately fifteen to twenty deer a season. In 1955, which was the last year we were in Ontario, we killed thirty-seven deer. We actually gave a lot of meat away to people on the lake who were short of food.

Orrah Jr. in front of five deer shot by him and Floyd. The horns on the last deer on the right were sawed off so that it could be hauled out of the woods.

We made all of our own oars and paddles out of spruce and jack pine with no knots, as planed wood will eventually split around a knot. We made our axe and hammer handles out of ash and oak. We bought axe heads, but the handles wore and broke after a while. We made all of our own snowshoes out of ash and birch crosspieces, using fawn hide for the webbing in the front and the rear. We used the neck of a buck for the bridge across the middle where your feet rest. The harness was made out of lamp wick or tanned heavy buckskin hide.

We made almost everything we used. We hardly bought anything. We built canoes out of cedar planking, which included heating up the sap off the cedar to bend it to make ribs. The heart of the cedar was used to make the planking. We used copper and brass nails to make the canoe. We bent the nosepiece out of ash and the gunwales out of spruce. Then we painted the outside of the canoe using three coats of marine paint.

We bought our traps from Fort Frances. We sold the fur to Neil Cathcart for years, until dad started the Ontario Trappers Association out of North Bay, Ontario. Dad was the president.

We made mattresses out of deer hair. We used the same techniques that mother had used for making feather robes to make the exterior of the mattress out of canvas.

We also made our own furniture. We made our own tables and benches using split white pine.

In the final analysis, we made it, grew it, hunted it, or did without.

Overcoming Seasickness—1938

We went over to Rabbit Island (Scotty Koocher's Island) which is straight south of Breezy Island on the American side. It was right after the Depression and just before the Second World War started. I went over there with my dad in what we called a gas boat with an antique Model T Ford engine in it. The waves were so high that they splashed on the broken coil system that it had and almost killed the engine several times. I was slightly seasick then, and I remember I was about six years old.

The only other time I got seasick was when I went down over Rainy in the old Whitney, which was a cargo-hauling boat used between International Falls and Kettle Falls. The waves had busted the wheelhouse. It had an ancient Buffalo engine in it. It was the boat used to run the commercially caught fish up to International Falls. They would make the round trip fish run from International Falls to Kettle Falls, going down one day and coming back up the next. They picked up all the fish from the commercial fishermen along the lakes. Scotty Koocher was driving, and when I was seven I went down to International Falls with my mother and got terribly seasick. I have never been seasick since.

Our First Boat—1939

In 1939, dad bought our first boat from Fred Lessard. The boat had originally belonged to a man in International Falls. The boat was named after the original Ironsides sailing ship. Dad had to pay duty on it to bring it across the border into Canada. It was thirty-five feet long with a Gardner engine. Dad eventually replaced the Gardner engine with a Model A Ford engine. It had no cabin on it, so he built one. Over time, the galvanized bottom rusted out as it was constantly being pulled up on the beaches in Northern Ontario.

Our family used the Ironsides for years. In 1956, it was loaded on the train and moved out to Prince Rupert, British Columbia. Before they left, Dad bought sheets of eight-by-four steel, which were shipped with the boat. After it arrived in Prince Rupert, Dad welded the sheets to the bottom. Then he treated the new bottom so that it never leaked again, even though it was used at sea. It made it to Ketchikan, Alaska, and up the Skeena River in British Columbia. The last time I heard of it operating was in 1962.

The Langfords

M r. and Mrs. Barney Langford lived about one mile from the Kettle River place. The Kettle River place had been a railroad tie camp, which my granddad, Frank Kielczewski, owned. The location made ties for railroad tracks. The Langfords raised ranch mink and had a commercial fishing ground. They trapped mink in the fall and muskrats in the spring. Mrs. Langford did most of the trapping.

The Langfords had an Edison cylinder phonograph. As children, we would go to visit, and we played her phonograph so much she eventually gave it to us to take home.

When I was nine years old, Mr. Langford (Barney) went to town for about two weeks. Mrs. Langford came and asked my mom and dad if I could go down to stay with her while Barney was away. No one was home with her as her son, Bert, was also away at the time.

Their home was at the mouths of Bear River and Hale Bay. The house was set about twenty feet off the cliff on the edge of the lake. Mrs. Langford and I snow shoed back to her home. I helped carry all the wood for the cook stove and helped her feed the mink. They had about one hundred ranch mink. We set a gill net under the ice by Hale Bay and another one near the mouth of Bear River. In Hale Bay we caught whitefish, bluefins, and suckers. We caught walleye and northern pike in the mouth of Bear River.

We cooked the fish and added it to meal, which we fed to the mink. The walleyes and whitefish we ate. We also had deer meat. I stayed there two weeks.

I remember that Rusty Meyers, who flew a fifty-horsepower Cub airplane that had skis on it, brought in the mayor from Fort Frances and landed at the Langfords'. They told me I could go down and look at the plane. It was the first time that I had seen a plane up close. After that I wanted to fly very much.

At one time, there was a bear denned up on the Langfords' island. The Langfords had wanted the bear disposed of because it kept coming around trying to eat the mink food. They were also concerned that the bear would kill the mink. When dad shot the bear, it slid back down into the den, so dad crawled into the den to drag it out. When he did so, he was bitten by one of the two cubs in the den. Realizing the cubs would not survive without the mother, he shot both of them as well. We rendered the bear grease off the large female bear, and our family ate the one cub. The other cub as well as part of the female we gave to the Langfords. We didn't have much lard at home, so the bear grease was very useful. Mr. Langford never called me by my given name. He always called me "Buddy." He would say, "What are you up to, Buddy?" I really liked the Langfords. They were always good to me.

While I was staying with Mrs. Langford, she taught me how to pray. She used to pray every night. Mrs. Langford's heritage was Eskimo, Native Canadian Indian, and French.

The Langfords had a sawmill carriage made by Bell. Dad took the steamboat down to the Langfords one summer and made a pattern of the sawmill carriage so that he could make his own. He constructed it out of angle and channel iron. We powered it with an antique Stanley car engine. We used it to cut the lumber for the house we built on the bank of the Falls River. We also sold some of that lumber to a resort located between Kettle Falls and the Langfords' on Gullboy Island.

The Langfords had four children. I remember Shorty, Bert, Artie, and a girl, Olive. Olive later worked at Bernardi's Grocery Store on Scott Street in Fort Frances. Our family bought groceries there for many years. The store was originally called Bellows.

Learning to Call Animals—1941

When I was seven or eight years old, I started calling loons, who would come right up to me and dive down and fish where I was fishing. I tried and tried until finally a loon came toward me. I was so excited about my success!

My dad taught me how to call geese and moose as well. I tried calling Canadian geese and finally mastered that. Later I learned to call both bull and cow moose by listening to them call to each other.

Eventually I learned how to call deer, hoot like an owl, and cry like a rabbit. I learned to imitate many wild animals.

One time Frank and I pulled our canoe under a bunch of brush on the Big Marsh. Geese were circling overhead, and I called them. We waited until they landed, and we got five of them in the dark. The next day, Frank shot two more. We lived off ducks and geese, as did the Indians in the area.

On another occasion, Frank was camping by himself on an island located on Connickson Lake when he heard a bull moose calling, so he answered like a cow. Eventually the bull came out of the woods and swam out to the island. When that bull realized that there wasn't any cow, he began stomping all over the point. The moose was knocking down dead trees three inches in diameter. Frank jumped into his canoe and shot the moose in the behind with number two shot. Frank was a good distance away, so it didn't hurt him. But the moose did leave the island

and swam back to the mainland. Frank said he could hear the moose talking to himself as he stomped away for at least three or four miles. Thankfully, the moose had not stomped all over his tent, which remained intact. Frank moved to another island just in case the moose came back. He didn't answer any more bull moose calls after that experience.

1952 – Frank at the Big Marsh Cabin holding a double barrel shotgun with a Damascus wire twist barrel made out of haywire. Frank is standing in front of Floyd's canoe with one of the sled dogs, Sandy, at his feet.

Making a Living—1941

In 1941, my dad received a permit from J. A. Mathieu's in Fort Frances to pick logs on the US and Canadian border. In 1945, he still had clearance for Namakan Lake and the US border.

I was thirteen years old, and the war had just ended. We picked logs on both the American and Canadian sides of Namakan Lake. J. A. Mathieu had a new houseboat built. His original houseboat was for sale. It was a beautiful houseboat made out of knotty pine. It was two stories high, fifty feet long, and fourteen feet wide. It had a veranda all around it. The houseboat was twenty feet wide including the veranda, with a wraparound railing. It had an electric ice shed, a thousand-watt generator, and eight rooms on the first floor, which included bedrooms, a kitchen, and a living room at the front of the houseboat. The hull itself had a two- or three-inch plank on the bottom, which kept the houseboat afloat. The walls were six inches wide and lathe built, making it difficult to repair.

In order to purchase the houseboat, we trapped beaver. During beaver season, we were allowed ten beaver per person. In addition, we went ahead and trapped for J. A. Mathieu. He wanted us to trap live beaver for his pond west of Fort Frances out toward Emo, Ontario.

In 1946, when I was fourteen years old, I was left alone up at the homestead on the Falls River. My parents went up to Red Gut to pick logs. My uncle Allen would come down to keep me company on occasion. His fishing grounds came down as far as the mouth of Stokes Bay. He had gill nets set there, so when he tended his nets, he would come down and stay overnight with me, bringing along fresh fish to eat. I was there by myself except when he came to visit.

I learned how to handle beaver with my bare hands, and I learned to respect them and their teeth. I saw what they could do to one another with their teeth. We had them in cages, and one of them bit another because he got mad at him. We ended up having to kill the wounded one because he was so badly hurt. He had been bitten on the shoulder and it went right through the bone. We had them in wooden cages back up in the woods. We killed and pelted those that had broken legs or were badly injured and sold the pelts to the senior M. T. Cathcart.

1946 – The Wee George towing the houseboat purchased from J. A. Mathieu. Floyd's mother, Violet, and his sister, Elnora, are standing at the back of the houseboat.

1946 – The houseboat purchased from J. A. Mathieu. Floyd's uncle, Paul Kielczewski, is standing on the second floor of the houseboat.

I really enjoyed being able to take animals alive and not have to kill them. I liked seeing young beaver. We took out pairs as well, female and male together. J.A. Mathieu started a beaver farm out at his pond and bought live pairs of beaver from my dad to populate it. My dad told him, "Those beaver are going to multiply, Mr. Mathieu, and we are going to have to come out there and shoot them for you." However, Mr. Mathieu wanted those beaver real bad. We gave them to him, and those beaver started chewing up everything around them and damming up his pond. They chewed up all of his trees. In time, he asked us to come back and shoot the beaver. But we told him we didn't have the heart to come out and shoot them after we had taken them alive.

We picked logs for J. A. Mathieu for seven or eight years. That was our summer income at that time.

That was before I went into guiding. I started guiding at fifteen years old. At the time, you were supposed to be sixteen in order to get a guide's license. I lied about my age in order to get the license. I made a living guiding in the summertime and trapping in the winter. That was our income back in the early days up on Rainy Lake, the Pipestone River, Namakan Lake, and that area of the country.

Floyd's dad is holding beaver that still need to be skinned while Floyd is holding up a beaver hide that has already been skinned.

1946 – Floyd at 14 years old at the Falls River homestead with the fur from animals he trapped. He has an otter on his head while holding up mink with two fox; one on each arm.

1953 - Floyd at the Big Marsh Cabin with beaver he had just caught that morning.

It was a good experience but very hard. It wasn't easy. I remember that several times we did not have much food to eat. I remember going hungry.

In 1941, Orrah Jr. was eleven years old and I was nine. We were alone at the Kettle Falls shack trying to catch fish using seaman's twine and a hook. We caught some rock bass and perch. Our uncle Paul stopped by in his boat and gave us some food. Paul stayed and cooked a meal for us, too.

I vowed when I was a young boy growing up that I was going to become a good hunter and a good shot. I did become one of the best at that time. Eventually I made *Outdoor Life* and *Boone and Crockett* magazines. In addition to the hide, I have the skull of the big bear, which just missed qualifying for *Boone and Crockett* by not even a quarter of an inch. *Boone and Crockett* goes by the skull size and not the hide. That bear was about fifteen years old. Their life span is generally between twenty-five and thirty-five years. I have heard of some living to fifty years old, but not very often.

One of the bears my dad killed at Moose Camp Creek was so old that it only had one or two teeth left. All of the cutters between the big fangs were worn off and gone. The grinders in the back were worn right down to nothing. Dad figured it was about thirty-five years old. It had been caught in several Indian timber wolf snares, but it had managed to get out of them. It had no hair around its neck. Instead of hair, there was a caul of scar tissue two inches thick from where it had pulled itself out of snares.

The Beaver Dam Bear—1941

In 1941, World War II had just started. I was nine years old when I went along with my dad and mother to scout out a trap line that was fourteen miles long and ten miles wide. At that time, I think we said it was around 140 square miles.

We started out late in December, when everything was frozen up. We slept in tents and sometimes we just slept out in the open under the stars. My mother made feather robes with duck feathers. They were eight feet wide by ten feet long. We took two feather robes each, one for the bottom and one for the top. She would pocket them into rows and sections. We could sleep in temperatures of sixty below zero without getting cold. The pillows were made from rough grouse and partridge feathers as they were not as warm as duck but they made a good pillow.

We built doghouses on the trap line during the fall for the dogs to stay in during the winter. The doghouses had hay beds, and burlap gunnysacks, which hung over the doors.

We traveled to Pipe Lake by dogsled. We had five dogs on that trip. Five dogs make a nice team. We made the dog food from bran shorts, fat, and fish, and then we froze it and took it along to feed them.

Mother drove the dog team, and dad cleared the trail ahead of the sled, while I ran behind. We weren't traveling very fast because we were scouting out new territory. I was the only child they took along. The others stayed at the home place, and Wes, the oldest, was looking after Orrah Jr., Frank, Elnora, Violet, and Tony. Wes was only twelve years old at the time.

Floyd's dad and his brothers, Frank and Tony, in a homemade tent, which was used while trapping beaver on the Pipestone River in the spring of the year just before the ice went out. These homemade tents were used in the years before the cabins were built by Wes and Floyd.

We came to a lake we called Crescent Lake because it was shaped like a crescent; the map called it Mohan Lake. I remember telling my dad to "look at the big beaver house in the middle of those jack pines." The lake appeared to be dammed up to about four feet.

Years later, my dad and I had the opportunity to talk to an Indian fellow who had staked that house off. He told us they staked off the beaver's food, used snares and ladders, and caught twenty-six beaver from that great big house. They believed they captured all the beaver. Old Gilbert Ashway, Chief of the Lac La Croix Indians on Lac La Croix, verified that they caught them with the snares. It was a huge house, which had many compartments.

We came back to the area several years later to trap not far from that ancient beaver house. Dad and Frank were talking about the bear that was living in the beaver house now. The dam had washed out, and the bear denned up in that beaver house, and now it had a big jack pine growing out of the top. In my mind's eye, I can still see that tree and that beaver house today. I will never forget that as long as I live.

I had shot a number of bears in snares and in traps, but I'd never shot one that wasn't encumbered. Frank and I used to practice shooting at moving targets by throwing something up in the air pretending it was a bear.

We would say, "Did you get it?" and if the response was no, we would say, "Oh, the bear got you."

Dad used to ask us, "What would you do if a bear charged you?" I told him I'd shoot him. Then dad would say, "No you wouldn't; you would just faint."

My dog, Sandy, was hurt by a bear, and I was telling dad about how Sandy was scared of bears because he had been crippled by one. A big bear had swatted him on the hip. I figured he must have gone to play with the cubs and the mother bear crippled him. He wasn't scared of timber wolves, but he sure was afraid of bear.

Frank and my dad kept asking me, "Did you know that there's a bear in that beaver house up there, Floyd?" I told them that I didn't know for sure and suggested we go take a look. Frank told me, "Take my old 38-55 Carbine, and shoot that bear." I told him that I would.

Then I asked dad, "What are you going to do?" He told me matter-of-factly, "I will shoot him."

I told him, "That bear will run over the top of me and be gone a mile before your gun ever leaves the leather."

Dad said, "Oh, no, it won't." But I bet him it would. Dad became a bit leery then, but he continued talking about the bear. The beaver house had shrunk down; there was no water around it. We just walked up from ground level to the top. It was a nice dry beaver house, which made a great bear den.

Dad didn't want me to cock the hammer on the 38-55 because he was afraid that I'd accidentally shoot him while he was standing on top of the house.

I said, "You mean I have to take aim, cock the hammer, and then shoot that bear?"

He said, "Yeah, that's right." Dad was about ten feet from me on top of the beaver house.

Like I said, the house was old and settled on the ground. Tree roots were growing through it that were about eight to ten inches in diameter. When the beaver lived there those same roots had been only about four or five inches in diameter. It had grown that much in the years since I first saw it.

I was standing in front of the bear's tunnel. My dad was atop the house, where he had drilled a hole with a tag alder. He was prodding the bear through the hole with the tag alder. I could see through the tunnel that the bear was moving.

I said, "I see him moving, I see him moving." Then all of a sudden, all I could see was brown and a cloud of dust, and that the bear was charging me. He was moving fast. I cocked the hammer on Frank's Winchester, an old ninety-four model, and took aim as quickly as I could. I hit him an inch above his eye. I jumped about four feet off the ground. The empty cartridge was in the air, and I was ready to shoot again, but he was already dead. He fell to the ground, his nose sliding into the snow. I could see the steam coming out of his nose.

Dad said, "Uh, oh, that did it!"

I said, "See, you didn't even get your gun out of the holster. That thing would have run over the top of me and would have been two miles away before you ever got the gun out of your holster!"

I guess my reaction had showed him that I wouldn't faint.

Dad said, "You moved like a bolt of lightning. Well, boy, you proved yourself!"

It wasn't a big bear, only about 150 pounds. But it was still big enough to maul someone.

I brought my dog, Sandy, over to see the dead bear. He was scared, but I slowly broke him of that. After that experience, he understood we could kill them. When the big bear broke into the cabin on Pipe Lake, Sandy was ready to fight.

Is It a Loon or a Goose?

I was about nine years old, and the Second World War had just started. My brother, Wes, and I went to Falls Lake up on the Falls River. Dad had built an A-frame to support a tent up there where we stayed. It didn't have any walls, but the stove in it kept it warm. Dad hauled the lumber up from McKenzie Point.

The lake was frozen, but the bay near the river was open. A loon had landed there, but he couldn't get back in the air because he did not have enough open water to take off. A loon needs more open water to take off in than a duck or goose. Geese and ducks can lift right off the water. The loon was feeding in the open water.

Wes and I didn't have much food, so I called the loon. We took our well-worn red skiff out onto the water. Wes shot at it, thinking it was a goose. He broke his wing, so he couldn't fly. The bird dove but had to come up for air. When it came back up, Wes shot it in the head. My brother still thought it was a goose, but I knew it was a loon. He roasted it on a spit over an open fire. I really couldn't say it tasted fishy because I was so hungry, I didn't care.

We had about half of it left when Dad came up about a day later. He looked at it and said, "Boy, it doesn't look like a goose." He ate some of it and said, "It doesn't taste like a goose." Then he went around the back of the cabin and saw the loon's head and feathers. Dad said, "That is no goose. That is a loon!"

Our position was that it couldn't have been any worse than eating a snapping turtle.

Trapping on Beaver House Creek

During the Second World War, in 1943 and 1944, we were up on what we called Beaver House Creek off of Steward Lake. The beaver had made Beaver House Creek about a hundred years prior. We knew this because the Jack Pine growing out of the middle of the dam was twenty inches in diameter and over thirty feet tall. I don't think there was a creek there before the beaver damned it up. We named it Beaver House Creek because the beaver had built it. It was not even on the map.

My dad, Wes, Orrah Jr., and I had built a lean-to and carpeted it with spruce and balsam boughs. We put up horizontal poles. If you laid boughs down like a feather starting from the bottom and going to the top and then put a tarp on top of that, any water, rain, or snow would shed off. We had a big fire in front of us. The first time we had a lean-to with a tarp over us, the temperature dropped to between forty and forty-five below zero. We slept under the feather robes my mother made with a carpet of boughs under us and were quite comfortable. I remember holding our tin plates over the fire to eat our food because it would literally start freezing if it was away from the fire. We washed our hands in the snow. We couldn't chop holes in the creek because it was frozen right down to the bottom. We got up there by dog team. We hauled flour, baking powder, salt, lard, potatoes, onions, carrots, and rutabagas. We kept the vegetables in our sleeping bags with us to keep them from freezing. We only ate two meals a day: breakfast and supper. We fed the dogs venison from deer caught in wolf snares. It was an absolutely beautiful lake. There was an old trapping cabin on the northwest corner that had fallen in. It was at least fifty years old then. There was an axe stuck in a tree, with the handle rotted out of it, and the tree had grown up around the blade of the axe. It was then that I realized that trees grow from the top and not from the bottom. The axe must have been in the tree for about forty years. We set traps there in the winter for beaver, mink, otter, fox, wolves, or any fur-bearing animal that we could get. We would even sell a bear hide if we trapped a bear. There was no martin or fisher in those days. I saw the first martin track about 1953. They just started showing up then. A martin is also called a sable. A martin is smaller, faster, and prettier than a fisher. The first fisher I caught was in 1953. I got five of them: the male, the female, and three kits. A fisher is similar to a wolverine and is about as vicious as well. A martin's face is similar to a fox's.

Wes, Frank, Floyd, and Orrah Jr. Wes is holding a wolf hide while Floyd is holding a coyote hide with many beaver hides surrounding them.

Daylight—1943

About two years into the war, we were picking up logs on Rainy Lake for the J. A. Mathieu Lumber Company. We also picked logs belonging to the Virginia and Rainy Lake Lumber Company and Shevlin-Clarke Company, which J.A. Mathieu had the franchise rights to. Those companies were on the American side, and we had a permit to pick both sides of the border during the war. We took anything stamped with J.A. Mathieu's name, Virginia and Rainy Lake Lumber Company or Shevlin-Clarke. We'd row out to a stray log, nail the steel dog into the log, and run a three-inch cable through the steel dog's eye. We hooked the stray logs together on that cable and eventually had a raft of logs we towed behind us. We'd tow the raft to the log boom, knock all the dogs out, and add the tow to the boom. A boom is created with chains circling the logs. Each boom had at least a double chain. We towed the boom down to the mill using our steamboat. A standard-sized log is about twenty-four inches across and sixteen feet long. The last year we picked logs was 1945, and our tow included 1,700 logs. We picked logs off Rainy and Namakan Lakes on both sides of the border and sleuthed them through the Canadian dam at Kettle Falls.

When I was nine or ten, I used to hate to see daylight come. I could read steam before I could tell time. Reading steam means looking at the pressure gauge on the boiler. As the pressure gauge goes up it shows in pounds, so if you had 140 pounds of steam, that would be a full head of steam. We never wanted it to go much higher than that because the pop-off valve would pop and let steam out of the boiler so it wouldn't blow up. If that valve didn't let enough steam out, then the boiler could blow up since steam expands. We always had to be reading the steam and have an action plan for managing the pressure to keep it at 140 pounds. If there wasn't enough pressure, the engine wouldn't run hard enough at full throttle. We had to have at least 125 pounds of pressure to run the steam engine when we were towing logs.

My dad had an ancient steamboat called The Wee George. The George family out of Atikokan and Fort Frances built it. The Georges had put a boiler in it from the old Canadian Dam at Kettle Falls. This steamboat used to be the passenger hauler that traveled between International Falls and Lake of the Woods through Rainy River. They called it The Rambler. It was a small boat and sat very low. I remember being in some awful storms in it. We almost sank a couple of times, but we managed to stay afloat.

During the summer, up in Northern Ontario, we rowed and picked up logs sometimes until nightfall, which didn't come until eleven at night, and dawn came at four o'clock in the morning. I usually went to bed at dark and was called on when it was just breaking dawn.

The Bear with Two Lives or Don't Shoot a Bear with a .22—1944

In the spring of 1944, we were trapping up on Rainy Lake. I was twelve years old. I set up a trap for muskrats using aniseed oil, dried apple and hay strung from a tripod over a trap. When a muskrat jumped up to get the food, it got trapped.

Going up there, I saw big bear tracks along the river, and I was kind of scared. I was telling dad about it, and he said "Oh, that's all right. Don't worry about it. I'll go and tend those traps."

I told dad, "You better take a big gun with you because I am worried about that bear. It is a big bear." He did take his 30-40 Craig with him.

As dad approached in his canoe, he saw a big bear sitting on the point eating grass. Bear's back teeth are grinders, and they grind grass just like a cow. He was sitting there grinding away.

Dad paddled up to him and yelled. The trap dad was going to check was just on the other side of the bear. The bear didn't pay any attention to dad.

Then dad paddled up to within thirty yards of the bear and yelled, waving his jacket in the air. He had his 30-40 Craig with him, and he put the safety on halfway so that he could move it quickly over to the off position. He put the Craig down between his knees and took out the .22 Mossberg, which he had bought in Winnipeg. It was a fifteen-shot semiautomatic. He aimed right behind the bear's ears and pulled the trigger. He put seven shots in a circle in his neck. Dad said the bear took off with a loud snort and threw a puff of tender grass that landed in dad's canoe. Once the bear was gone, dad tended the traps. The bear kept on going, just a-snorting and a-woofing and talking to himself.

A couple of years later in the same area I set a bear trap. I caught a buzzard and a wolf in it, and then I caught a bear.

We were going to be gone for about five days, so when we got to my granddad's place, I asked him to check on my bear trap. He said he would. When we got back, granddad said, "Oh! Did you ever catch a big bear, Floyd!" Then he said, "But an even bigger one killed your bear by crushing his head, and then that bear ate yours." The older bear killed the younger one because he was a competitor in his territory.

My dad and I went back up to reset the trap. We reset the Blake and Lamb 415 bear trap using the bear carcass as bait. We used a six-foot Elm toggle that was about four inches in diameter. We sharpened hazel bush branches and placed them around the trap so that when the bear stepped on them he would quickly move his feet off of the sharp branches and into our trap.

We often set the traps with sharp hazel brush or willow limbs, sharpened on both ends. Once they were sharpened, we would shove one end into the ground with the other end of the sharpened limb sticking up out of the ground. We then covered the sharpened ends that were sticking up with hay. Then we set the trap on an angle with the jaws crossways so the bear's foot would be caught. I caught that big bear because dad showed me how to set a bear trap. Dad said an older Indian, Abby Knot, who lived up on the Bear River on Frankfurt's Island, taught him how to set a bear trap.

We heard shots from the Falls River, so we went back there. Mother had shot at a deer swimming in the river but missed it. Later that same evening, dad had been thinking about the trap we'd set and said he knew that he set the ambush too close to the trap, so we went back to fix it. By the time we got there, the bear had already reached over the ambush, grabbed the carcass, and sprung the trap. Dad could hear the bear, which had been caught in the trap by two toes on his front foot. The bear was mad. He had chewed through the thick woods all around him fifty feet in diameter. Dad shot him once between the eyes with a forty-one-gauge Swiss rim fire rifle with a 340-grain bullet.

We rendered the fat off that bear, roasted him, brined him, made bacon out of him, and roasted the neck. We found seven .22 long rifle bullets in a circle right behind his ear, lodged two inches into his neck. It was the same bear that Dad had shot a couple of years earlier.

That experience taught me a lesson: to never shoot a bear with a .22 unless you are lucky enough to catch him with his head tipped down, and then you have to shoot him no more than one inch above the eyes. If its head isn't tipped down, it will just glance off and stun him, making him really mad.

Learning to Run White Water—1944

My dad helped me build a twelve-foot skiff that I used to run the rapids on the Pipestone River when I first started running white water at twelve years old. The following year, when my brother Frank was nine, he started going with me. After that, Frank and I were together always.

Wes, Orrah Jr., and I became expert canoeists. Dad taught us how to read white water. This entailed learning why the water swirled in places and made waves around rocks, where the current ran, and where the water was calm. I really liked running white water, took to learning it, and enjoyed the challenge.

Late 1950s – Hay Rapids on Namakan Lake.

Late 1950s – Floyd running Hay Rapids.

The Bears along Marsh Creek—1944

We had a tent on the Marsh Creek that we used for years. We put it up every year in September in preparation for the winter trapping season. The first time we put the tent up, I was twelve years old. Later on, we built a cabin in the same place. Since the tent did not have a floor, we were able to use a box stove that was about eighteen inches wide and thirty inches long with a lid on top and a damper. It sat right on the ground. We put sand all around it to prevent a fire from breaking out and burning down the tent. The tent was 16 by 12 feet with no floor.

My dad had forgotten a snare that he had set for wolves. He went up to get it; however, a big bear had gotten caught in it. He chewed every tree around him while caught. He chewed a jack pine log, which had fallen near him into bits. He broke the snare off and was gone by the time we got there. The bear had broken the snare off about a day before we arrived. It really scared me when I saw what the bear had done to the forest around him.

Along the cliff edge of Marsh Creek, the whole area was covered with jack pines. The cliff was about sixty feet above the creek. The bears had chewed all the jack pines along the edge of the creek, marking their territory. That country was thick with bear. The chewing had caused the pitch to run out, which killed the trees. We took an axe and chopped down the dead bear-chewed trees and used them for firewood.

The jack pines were slivered thin from the bears chewing on them, so we cut off the dead portions and used them for kindling. We used the softer jack pine pitch, mixing it with pine tar to patch our canoes. We added lard to the pitch and used it as bug repellant on the dogs' ears and noses so the flies wouldn't chew their ears up.

1952 – Floyd and his dad at the Big Marsh Cabin with beaver and beaver hides.

The Falls River Bear—1945

My brother Frank was nine and I was thirteen years old when my dad came to visit us. We had pitched camp up on the Falls River only about four miles from the Falls River homestead. Frank and I were up there preparing for the fall trapping season. In order to get back to the homestead, we had to walk through a three-mile strip of thick, almost impenetrable woods, and then there was about a mile and a half of water where we had to paddle a canoe the rest of the way down the Falls River to the homestead. Dad came up to visit us and see how we were doing. Frank came running into the tent and said to dad and me, "I see a big bear track down the path here."

I said, "Oh, I don't know if he saw a bear or not." So I walked the trail, and sure enough, there was a big bear track right over dad's tracks. This meant that the bear had come by in the short time that dad had been visiting.

The three of us had gone upriver earlier that day, and dad shot a mallard. Dad left but told us that the bear might come back. That night, about nine o'clock or so, I cleaned the mallard and cooked it with some beans for the next morning. The bear must have smelled that cooking.

The only light we had was from an aged coal oil kerosene lantern with a wick and oil in the bottom. It was painted red, and I still remember it to this day.

Dad told us that he didn't think the bear would bother us, but just in case he said, "I'll leave you this sixteen-gauge shotgun." It held two shots: one in the magazine and one in the barrel.

Then dad said, "If he comes back, wait till he is close, and cut a ring into the shell just above the wad, so that the whole wad goes out with the charged shot, so it acts like a bullet." Dad left soon after.

I didn't have time to ring the shell, but I did have the gun ready. I figured if he got close enough, I would just blow his head off. Later that evening we heard a noise outside that sounded like someone clearing his or her throat. I called out, "Is that you, dad?" No answer. And then I heard the noise again. I pulled the tent flap back while Frank held that old lantern. We looked in the direction of the noise but didn't see anything. Pretty soon we heard a whining noise and the sound of a bear jaw smacking.

I said, "That is not dad, Frank. That is not dad. That is a big bear."

We saw his shadow in the dim lantern light; he was sitting on his haunches about thirty feet away.

I had already taken the safety off, and I threw a piece of stove wood at him. It made a whooshing sound as it sailed through the air. He let out a loud "woof" when he jumped out of the way. The wood landed right where he had been sitting.

We were worried because we didn't know what he was going to do next. We could hear him take off toward the northwest. Then we heard him crashing through the brush, and every so often we heard him let out a loud moan and work his jaws. I knew then that he was upset and that he wanted food. We didn't have any flashlights back then, which made it impossible to shine a light on something and shoot it. I remember going to bed and asking God to protect us. I think Frank and I were both surprised when we woke up the next morning.

We left the camp the next day. When we got back to the homestead, we told our dad. We had to go up to Fort Frances, so it was another five days before we were able to go back up to the camp. Dad was really horrified when he saw the camp and how everything was torn up. He could not believe it. The bear must have come back right after we had left. He had torn through one side of the tent and out the back. He chewed up all of our dishes and cups. The dishes were metal pans in those days, and the cups were made of tin. Dad figured he must have slept in the tent for at least three days. In time, the bear would have killed us because we were only children, and the bear knew that. The only chance we would have had was to catch him off guard, but that wasn't likely.

Dad said, "Good thing you guys left when you did. That bear might have killed you."

I was surprised when he said that. Dad was never worried about bear, but he was clearly worried this time. That is one experience that I will remember as long as I live.

1949 - Tony and Orrah Sr. in a canoe on the Falls River.

Seven Tornadoes—1945

One summer, when I was about thirteen years old and my brother Frank was nine, he and I were camped on the Canadian Kettle River. My granddad, Frank Kielczewski, had an unused camp there, where he once made ties for the railroad. Frank and I were living in the old office.

Our family moved there in 1939. Frank and I were left to take care of the home place while the rest of the family was off collecting logs. I became real sick. I don't know if it was typhoid fever or what, but I was deathly ill.

I rowed myself over to the Langfords', and Bert Langford took me to my granddad's place on Rat River, where my uncle Allen was staying. My uncles Allen, Paul, and Alton, along with my grandfather, Frank Kielczewski, and Grandma K. (Frank Kielczewski's second wife, Annie Verse) all stayed at the mouth of the Rat River on Rainy Lake.

I stayed there for three days and didn't eat or drink anything because I was so sick. They wanted me to eat, but I remembered a man who had died at the White Pine Hotel in Fort Frances from eating a raw potato on an empty stomach after he hadn't eaten for three or four days. Grandma K. said he died because his stomach couldn't handle the food. I also remember that as a young boy, we had a dog team where one of the dogs, Flash, was caught in a wolf trap. We found Flash five days later. When my mom fed all the dogs that day, Flash died. The food killed him.

That really stuck out in my mind, and I was only about eight or so at the time. It really scared me to see a dog die so quickly, and that's when I realized that I had better not eat anything after I had fasted for five days.

Uncle Allen eventually took me up to Bear's Pass on the Seine River in a sawed-off canoe with a 1.5 horsepower Johnson motor. My folks were there picking logs. On our way up there, in the area we called the Friendly Passes, from Black Point to Brule Narrows, we counted seven tornado spouts that touched down on the water. I will never forget that because uncle Allen's eyes stuck out of his head. I could tell by the look on his face that he was worried. My eyes must have been as big as saucers.

Those spouts caused twenty-foot-high waves, cutting twisting swaths through the forest as they passed. We pulled in behind a big rock in one place and watched the spouts come out of the sky and twist across the lake. It seemed odd because it wasn't even windy. These spouts appeared to come out of nowhere. We pulled in to three different islands to watch them.

All we had on the cutoff canoe was an ancient single-cycle Johnson motor, so it wasn't very fast. It was not something that either Allen or I had ever seen before or since.

We finally arrived at Bear's Pass, and I was still very ill. I didn't eat for another seven days. At some point, I was so gaunt that I didn't dare eat any food. After ten days, my mother diluted milk three times, and I had that for one day. The next day, she only diluted it twice. And on the third day, I was able to drink the milk undiluted.

At the end of five days, I was able to eat solid food. I have never forgotten how sick I was. We never knew what made me so ill. Some said it was just a bad case of stomach trouble.

Uncle Allen went back to the Kettle River camp and picked up Frank and took him by boat to the Langfords'. Frank was only nine, and he stayed at the Kettle River camp all by himself for those few days. He stayed with the Langfords for the next couple of days until I was well enough to come back down to the camp at Kettle River.

Not an Easy Life—1946

Life was not easy during the early days of the war. We didn't have much to eat. Everything was rationed, including sugar. I remember putting lard on my bread and using salt on it. I was really happy to have that much because fat was a commodity back then. Later on we had corn syrup that we got by the gallon. We really thought we had the world by the tail when we had a gallon of corn syrup. We put it on our bread for jam in the early days when I was a boy growing up just after the Depression and during the war.

Life was very tough. It was a matter of survival. It wasn't anything like the way we live today; I think we have things far too easy. At least I do, in comparison to what I had as a little boy. I remember a situation back in 1946, just after the war...

I was about fourteen years old when Wes and I walked up to camp on Horseshoe Bend on the south side of the Pipestone River, about five or six miles from the Falls River homestead.

It was spring, and the river and creeks were rising from the melting snow. Our knees and ankles were swollen from wading through the partially thawed creeks. During that time, the only thing we had to eat was partridge, rough grouse, and rabbits, but there was no fat on them. It was right after the war, and we did not have a lot of anything, including grease.

So we took the canoe and went across the river to see if we could find something with fat on it. We thought we could find a bear, and sure enough we did. We came upon the tracks of a big bear that had just come out of his den. It was in April. We started to follow that big bear and found his droppings. The pile he left was six inches high and two and a half inches across. His track in the snow was six or seven inches wide and at least eight or nine inches long. There was a bear claw in one of the droppings, indicating that he had eaten another bear. He was going northwest.

When I saw that, I said, "Wes, we only have single-shot twenty-twos. If we had big rifles, we could go after him, but not that feller. I am not about to. We don't need fat that bad."

So we went back across the river. I found a groundhog's hole and set a trap and caught it. We rendered down the groundhog and used the grease to cook our meat. We were both getting skinny from eating only lean protein with no fat.

After that I never killed anything that I wasn't going to use. Before that I used to kill groundhogs any time I saw them. If it wasn't for that groundhog, we might not have survived. Following that experience, I realized that it was a matter of survival, and I left any animal alone to continue living if I wasn't going to use it. It was on that trip I had left a paddle sticking in the tag alders edgeways so it wouldn't warp. When I came back to get my paddle in the fall, it looked like it had been shot with a shotgun. A bear had smelled the human scent on it and chewed it into slivers.

During that same year, dad, Frank, and I were up on the Falls River. Dad was going to do some trapping and get things put up for the fall. Dad, Frank, and I went upstream and looked the area over because we planned on putting a cabin there. We put up a tent, which we used during the winter. We cut pine boughs before the snow fell and hauled in hay so the tents and camps were ready before winter's snows buried everything. Then it would become too difficult to haul anything to the camp.

Floyd hauling a canoe on a toboggan by dog sled. The canoe was handmade by Orrah Jr. Floyd hauled it 25 miles over the ice from the Falls River homestead to Pipe Lake to avoid having to portage it when the river was open. They used it to haul out fur bearing animals trapped during the spring of the year.

The only type of bedding we had were hay and pine boughs we had cut. The tent had three-foot walls and no floor. We put a ridgepole through the center of the tent so it was easy to shovel the snow off. The outer walls of the tent were banked hip-high with snow. Shoveling snow off the top kept it from collapsing, and the snow around the bottom half of the tent worked as insulation.

We made a box stove out of sheet metal that we riveted together and folded. That stove provided our heat. At night the temperature dropped anywhere from thirty-five to fifty degrees below zero, which was the standing temperature, not including wind chill. Even though we kept the fire going all night, I could hear the water start to freeze in the gallon cans filled with creek water.

Once we heard the water start to freeze, we knew the temperature was dropping. We knew we needed to get up and build up the fire.

We stayed there for three or four days at a time. We trapped beaver, mink, and otter. We sold the pelts to Mr. Cathcart, a fur dealer in Fort Frances. We were paid twenty-five dollars for each otter, twenty for each mink, and an average of fourteen dollars for every beaver. Those were good prices then. We used the money to buy food and put some money in the bank a little at a time.

Frank and Floyd holding up three wolves they shot on the Pipestone River. Frank is holding the 30/03 British Ross 30 caliber with a bolt action and a straight pull. Due to over population, the Canadian government offered a $25.00 bounty. An additional $10.00 or $15.00 could be made by selling the hide.

Bears: Don't Love 'Em, Don't Hate 'Em—1946

I was fourteen when my folks left me alone to tend to the homestead on the Falls River while my dad and the rest of the family went up on the Red Gut River to pick logs. The Red Gut flows into Rainy Lake and originates from the Turtle River.

I was by myself, staying in a wanigan on the water. A wanigan is a raft, which has an enclosure built on it that is outfitted with a cook stove and is used primarily to store food supplies, cook and eat. Sometimes, they were outfitted with bunks to accommodate sleeping as well. Wanigans were used by logging companies to feed the logging crews as they floated logs down river to the mill. The wanigan had everything I needed, including a cook stove and bunk beds. My uncle Allen lived up on the Rat River, which was about nine miles away. When he was gill net fishing off the mouth of Stokes Bay he would bring me freshly caught fish.

Allen would come to camp in an open boat with a ten- or twenty-five-horsepower motor. He'd come about every three days or so, stay the night, and leave early the next morning.

Although it was illegal at the time, my family planned on raising live beaver. Live black beaver fetched a good price. I caught a small one alive, which we called Blackie. Because it was unlawful to keep them, we set a tent up in the woods on the other side of the Falls River across from the homestead where we kept the beaver.

Before my parents left for Red Gut, they wanted Frank to go over and stay with the beaver, but I said, "No. A bear will come over there and eat Frank along with the beaver." So Frank went up to Red Gut along with my parents. Every day I would go across the river to the tent to feed the beaver and give it water.

We had a tent pitched over the square beaver cage in which I put fresh hay for bedding. I always worried that someday I'd run into a bear up there, and all I had was a single-shot .22 rifle.

Sometime after my family returned, I went back to check on my beaver and saw that a bear had come in through the side of the tent and tore it down. I was surprised to see that the bear ripped the cage's wire netting away as though it was nothing. It was nearly a sixteenth of an inch wire netted cage, and the bear had torn that apart like it was made of Popsicle sticks.

Then he killed the little beaver and ate it. All I saw was its blood where he ripped it out of the cage. We intended to get a permit to raise beaver, but after the bear ate this one, we gave up on the idea.

Because we were breaking the law, I never said anything to uncle Allen about the beaver or the loss of it. Years later I told him what had happened. But that incident scared me real good. I guess that's why I am not a bear lover. I'm not a bear hater either; I just don't let them get in my way. Not anymore.

So don't tell me about bear. I have had my fill of them... breaking into cabins, tearing up canoes, chewing up paddles, and everything else they've done over the years.

I don't like bears, but if I can let a bear go, I do. I don't just deliberately kill them.

So yes, you're right. I am not a bear lover.

Cubby

Once my father was tending traps when he came upon a set, and all he saw was the tip of a bear's nose. The bear jumped up, and Dad shot it but only stunned it because the bullet ran up along the skull and didn't penetrate it. It was then that Dad saw he had caught a cub in the wolf trap by the nose. Dad looked all around for the mother bear, and when he didn't see her, he put the cub in a gunnysack and brought him home. We called him Cubby.

The cub never did take to my dad, but he liked my mother. He would call "mama, mama" when the dogs jumped on him. My mother would take a broom and chase the dogs away. The dogs used to beat him up, and then when he got older, he beat the dogs up.

We salvaged empty wooden barrels from a deserted logging camp. They were made of oak and were great for salting meat or as water barrels because they didn't leak. Cubby would sit on top of one of those wooden barrels thumping his feet and challenging the dogs to come and fight him. If the bear misbehaved, mother would take after it with a mop. To this day, I can still hear him bellowing.

My mother took care of the bear until it was two and a half years old. By that time it was getting dangerous. Dad was kind of worried about it too. Its collar was fraying, so one day Dad told us to let it go. We did, but it kept coming back and hanging around.

Most of us had gone to Oak Island and were picking blueberries. Mother, Elnora, and Wes were at the homestead. Mother worried that if the bear were hungry it would kill one of the little children. Elnora was only a baby, and mother was afraid that it would attack and kill Elnora. So she asked Wes, who was only twelve, to shoot it, which he did with mother's Marlon lever action.

They never said anything about it, not even to my dad. My mother told me this story when she was much older, just a few years before she passed away.

Building Trapping Cabins—1948

In January of 1948, nineteen-year-old Wes, and I, sixteen, were building trapping cabins. We built three cabins on the Pipestone River, one every seven miles. The first one was seven miles from home, which was the Poplar Cabin. The second one was built on the Big Marsh, which was fourteen miles from the homestead and seven miles from the Poplar Cabin. The Big Marsh Cabin was built out of jack pine and spruce. The third cabin was another seven miles from the Big Marsh Cabin, and it was located at the headwaters of Pipe Lake. Wes and I took the dog team up to build cabins along the trap line in places where we had previously used tents.

My brother Wes was really good with an axe. We split poplar in half using a wedge. Since it was so cold, they split very easily. We put poles down for a floor and put a split roof on top. We didn't use any nails in the roof except for the gabled ends.

Near Pipe Lake, we did not realize the current had undercut the ice beneath the snow. Wes was walking ahead of the dog team and me testing the depth of the ice with an axe. Not more than twenty feet later, he fell into the river up to his waist. It was thirty degrees below zero at the time. He hung onto his axe when he went through the ice, so he reached out with the axe and drove it into a solid piece of ice in front of the hole he had fallen into. In doing so, he was able to pull himself out of the freezing water. Wes's quick thinking to save himself was reflective of his skill with an axe. To date, I have not met anyone better than he with an axe.

We made camp right away on the shore, where I built a roaring fire and got him dry socks and underwear. We cut pine boughs to put on top of the snow so we could pitch our tent, and we built a fire in the four-gallon can we used as a stove. We cut more pine boughs for the dogs to lie on.

Wes's pants were frozen but dried out overnight hanging inside the tent. The next day we continued building the cabins.

Once the three cabins were finished, we returned home. It took us three weeks to build the three cabins.

At the end of October 1948, Orrah Jr. and I went up to finish the cabins. We chinked the roofs, put asphalt on them, built double bunks, and cut boughs and hay for mattresses. We gathered ferns to cushion the boughs and hay. We spread the sheets that mother had made over our homemade mattresses. Mother also had made us all ten-by-eight-foot feather robes so that two people could sleep under one if they had to. We put a thirty-gallon barrel stove in the Poplar Cabin and fixed it with a pipe damper on top and a damper in the bottom.

We had a floor in the Poplar Cabin but not in the Marsh Cabin or the Pipe Lake Cabin. The Marsh Cabin had a box stove that sat on the ground. The Pipe Lake Cabin had four bunks in it, an airtight stove, and a regular box stove, which we had bought from Winnipeg. It was a regular manufactured tent stove. The Poplar Cabin had a barrel stove, which we used for both cooking and heating the cabin. The Poplar Cabin was eighteen by sixteen, the Marsh Cabin was eighteen by fifteen, and the Pipe Lake Cabin was twenty by sixteen. Orrah and I built everything and finished it up so that it was ready for the trapping season that winter.

1953 – Floyd's brother, Frank, and his parents, Orrah Sr. and Violet, at the Pipe Lake Cabin. Violet is holding a beaver hide while Frank and Orrah Sr. are holding some of the 100 muskrats they caught. During the year, they took 1,000 beaver and 950 muskrats. The muskrats sold for between $2.50 and $2.75 each.

We built four doghouses at each one of the cabins. They were little A-frames with gunnysacks covering the doorways. We split the gunnysacks down the middle so the dogs could get in and out easily. We put lots of boughs and hay in there for the dogs. We shoveled the snow out from the front of the doghouses so that they wouldn't track snow into their beds, keeping them warm and dry. We were going to bed at dark, getting up at four in the morning, and starting work by daybreak. When we were finished, we left before daybreak and walked west along the big ridges, past the Poplar Cabin, twenty-four miles back to the homestead in one day. The ice on the river was only about an inch thick, so we couldn't walk on it. We had to take the big ridges back right through the woods using our compasses to get home. It took us twelve hours to walk back.

1954 – Floyd's sister, Violet, at the Pipe Lake Cabin.

Lassie and Sandy, My Lead Dogs

Lassie, a Border collie, and Sandy, an English collie, were my lead dogs. They were both really smart.

Lassie, the Border collie, was the lead dog on my dog team for five years. I could tell Lassie to get an article of clothing (socks, for example) and she would retrieve them and bring them to me. Lassie was a good lead dog who knew exactly which trail to take to get home.

In January of 1950, we were running out of food. Frank and I hauled 1,700 pounds of food from Crilly, Ontario, to Stokes Bay, which was fifty miles. We hauled the food in on a toboggan with a dog team. I ordered the food from Nick Palmer in Crilly, who ordered it from Bellows Store in Fort Frances. It came up by rail on the "local," which was a train that ran once a day from Fort Frances. I went out to Crilly to pick it up. It was flour, sugar, lard, cases of canned food, and even eggs wrapped in down quilts to keep them from breaking. In three trips, with just three small dogs including Lassie, we hauled the 1,700 pounds of food—approximately 560 pounds each trip.

On one of those three trips, I left Crilly, Ontario, at 10:00 p.m. This was the second trip of the day. I didn't think it was going to be this late, but we needed to move the food before it froze. It was fifty-seven degrees below zero standing temperature, not including any wind chill factor. It was still out; there was no wind. I was eighteen years old, and Frank was fourteen. Each of us wore four pair of socks and a pair of moccasins, two pairs of long-legged underwear and two pairs of pants, two parkas, and double shirts. It had been such a cold winter that the river had frozen to the bottom. It was fourteen miles through the woods from Crilly to the Pipe Lake Cabin. On Pipe Lake, I realized that the dogs' eyes were freezing shut when I was walking ahead of them and they started to stray off the trail. Frank was driving the dogs. I had to go over and wipe the frost off the dogs' eyes. We were about three miles from the cabin.

I said to Frank, "It must be seventy-five below zero out here."

We arrived at the cabin at 1:00 a.m. Later I found out that it was sixty-two below zero standing temperature in Atikokan, Ontario. It is always warmer in a city than it is in the woods, so it probably was seventy-five below in the woods, as I thought.

One night, Lassie got into a dish of poison intended for mice. The poison had been mixed with deer grease, so it was appealing to the dog. The dog lay down by my bed and was dead by the time I woke up the next morning. I really liked that dog, and I cried when she died. Later my dad brought a male English collie home, and I named him Sandy. I was about twenty years old.

Sandy became very aware of the land around him. If I told him to stay by my mitts or packsack, he would stay there for several hours if needed. When I left Prince Rupert in 1956 to go back to Namakan Lake, Sandy lay out on the point from which I left. No matter how much the family called the dog to come off the point, he wouldn't. He eventually died there. He was seven years old. I should have built a crate and taken him back on the train with me.

1953 – Floyd skinning beaver with two of his sled dogs, Queenie and Sandy, beside him.

The Value of a Compass—1948

I was sixteen years old when I wounded a deer. It fell, got up, and took off. The gun I had was an ancient, rebuilt 38-55 rifle. It had been re-bored, and I was using hand-loaded lead bullets. We made the lead bullets ourselves with a reloading kit that Dad had bought. However, the kit did not come with copper jackets for the bullets. As a result, the bullets were a little small for the re-bored gun. Consequently, sometimes the bullets went straight, but other times they went end over end, and one time I found a bullet sideways in a deer I had shot. The gun was accurate, but the bullets were not.

On this occasion, I only nicked the deer on its back. I kept chasing the thing. It was snowing, and I kept following and following it. I'd get close enough and shoot at it but miss it. Pretty soon, as it got later, I thought, '*Well, I better go to the camp*' (where we had pitched a tent). The camp was straight to the south. I could just walk straight out to it. It would only be about a mile and a half.

When I took out the compass, I was heading straight north, and I couldn't believe I was heading straight north. I didn't want to believe the compass. It just didn't seem right. I turned around and went back and started south again. I stopped and looked at the compass, and again I was heading due north. So I thought it couldn't be right. I learned a lesson that day. I learned to believe the compass unless you are over an iron deposit. The magnetic draw of an iron deposit can cause a compass to be wildly inaccurate. I have been over that too, but you can get off it and find your course again.

I kept checking the compass, and pretty soon I was heading west. I finally came out about three miles below the tent. There was eight inches of snow on the ground. If I would have just followed the compass to start with, I would have been within less than a mile of the camp. I knew where I was when I came out of the woods on Marsh Creek because I recognized Marsh Creek. I could see what we called Falls Lake, which was Greer Lake on the map. I turned around and walked along the creek back up to the camp, which was almost a three-mile hike on the ice.

Until I came out on Marsh Creek, I had been completely lost, only because I didn't want to believe the compass. The snow had already filled my tracks, so I couldn't follow them back to the camp.

A day and a half later, I finally got the deer. I went back to where I had shot it, and I followed the drops of blood from the nick, and it was only just a nick. When I finally caught up with it, I could have thrown the gun at it, I was that close. Fortunately, the gun worked that time, so I shot it.

I had chased that deer for three days. I was so upset after chasing it for so long that when it stood up in its bed, I just poured the lead into it. I hit it four times.

This time I followed the compass and packed the deer straight out to the camp.

Trapping Under the Ice

My brother Orrah was the best under-the-ice beaver trapper I ever saw in my life. He could make sets, knew exactly where the beaver would put his foot, and could get the beaver to go right into it. He could take one hundred and twenty-five beaver from under the ice, per season, by himself. Each year he would start on the first of December, and by the fifteenth of March, he had taken his limit.

He would put the sets in the tunnel using a fork made from dry poplar, maple, or ash with a little number three trap. He'd put the trap crossways and tip it just so, making sure that it would catch the beaver by the foot. He took up to nineteen beaver out of one house. He said that he seldom missed one. The next best beaver trappers were my uncles Allen and Alton Kielczewski.

Allen taught me a lot about trapping under the ice, and I use those methods to this day. Seldom do I miss a beaver. For the past fifteen years, I have been working for the federal government trapping nuisance beaver. Whenever beaver dams threaten roads or when big beaver dams flood roads, I am called on to trap the beaver and remove them from the area.

1952 - Floyd's brother, Orrah Jr., with his dog team outside of the Pot Hole Lake Cabin.

Beaver trapping with a dog team and a single set trap on the left and a double set trap on the right. The double set trap is made to catch two beaver concurrently; one in each set.

84

A typical beaver caught under the ice by his left front foot using a platform set.

1953 – Orrah Jr. in front of the drying shed at the Falls River homestead with beaver he had caught under the ice.

Pothole Lake Cabin—1950

I was with Frank in a great big swamp, and the sun was going down. Moss grew on both sides of the trees, so you couldn't tell direction by it. We were headed for the Pothole Lake Cabin. We called it Pothole Lake because it was so small it wasn't on any of the maps. It was about eight miles straight south of the Pipestone River and was made by beaver damming it up.

Frank asked me, "What are we going to do?"

I told him, "We're going to use the compass." I headed straight south, believing the compass that time, and after two miles we walked out of the swamp, arriving dead center at the back of the cabin. The compass needle was pointed directly at the cabin ridgepole. We didn't vary our course, and I couldn't believe it when I hit the cabin dead center.

After that I went out many times at night using the stars, or the North Star, or just the moonlight as my guide, but I was always more accurate when I used the compass. There are three basic things you need for survival in the wilderness: a compass, a map, and waterproof matches or something else to build a fire with. You shouldn't go anywhere in the wilderness without these three tools.

My First Big Game Deer

Dad fixed up the Arisaka thirty-one caliber for me. Over time I killed fifty-six deer with it. This time, it was November, and Frank and I were staying up at the Kettle River Cabin, which was Granddad's old railroad tie camp office. I got up early one morning and left Frank at the cabin.

I wounded a big buck and chased him three miles across to Hale Bay, but I never got him. I realized that it was getting late and I needed to get back to the cabin. So I went back and had a bite to eat. When I was finished, I came out of the cabin, and not even three hundred yards behind the cabin was a ten-point buck. He was bedded down under the balsam because a storm was coming in. I surprised him, he jumped up, and I shot him but only cut some hair off the top of his back. He ran and I chased him. He was standing between two cedar trees, and all I could see were his horns sticking up over the top of his back. So I shot him through the middle near the top of his back with one shot, which killed him. Frank helped me shoulder him, and I packed him out in one piece. He was 225 pounds.

Frank and I loaded the deer in the well-used wooden Arrowhead boat with a 2.5-horsepower Johnson motor. The wind was howling, and the waves were ten feet high. It was getting dark so it was hard to see. As the waves rolled over the boat, Frank bailed water out. The water was freezing on the gunwales. I don't know how we made it back to the homestead on the Falls River. An inch and a half of ice froze on the Falls River that night, so solid you could walk on it. It also taught me a lesson about traveling in treacherous, freezing, windy weather and compounding the danger with a heavy load. We could have drowned. It got down to almost zero and froze so hard that night that we had to cut Wes's wooden boat out of the ice. Yet we had come in on open water. The water was freezing and scumming over as we came in with the deer.

I drained the motor, but not enough. The cylinders froze in it, which popped out the frost plugs in the ends, so at least the block didn't bust. The foot had grease in it, so it didn't hurt the foot.

Dad said, "You should have drained all the water out of it, Sonny." It was fortunate that it didn't hurt the motor. Motors back then had to be drained. It taught me a lesson about draining motors. The motors we have now drain automatically.

That was my first big game deer. The kind hunters dream of getting.

Floyd's first ten-point buck pictured in front of the houseboat at the Falls River homestead.

Never Shoot a Bear Just Once—1951

Frank was fifteen years old and staying at the Kettle River Cabin. I always told him, "Never shoot a bear just once." Dad had told us a story about a man out on the East Coast who shot a bear he thought was dead, and then it rose up and clawed him, nearly killing him. Frank was deer hunting at the Poplar Cabin by himself with the 38-55. He saw a track and thought someone had shot his deer and was dragging it out. As he came around the corner, he saw a bear dragging branches and leaves to make a den for the winter. He was denning up later in the fall than usual. It was a huge bear only fifteen feet from him. The bear rose up and started growling at him. Frank shot him three times quick, right between the eyes. There was lead right up to the bear's shoulder.

I told him, "Well, Frank, you didn't have to shoot him that much."

He said, "You remember what you told me…don't shoot a bear just once."

The bear had four inches of fat on him. It was a big one. I have the picture of the bear hanging in front of the Poplar Cabin. We rendered down a hundred pounds of fat off of that bear because fat was scarce in those days. The bear was close to five hundred pounds. It was a monstrous animal.

Deer in the Doghouse—1951

It was the winter of 1951 at the Poplar Cabin. The snow was about four feet deep, which was too deep for the deer to get through to browse on vegetation as they normally did in the winter. Typically, they ate hazel brush tips, cedar boughs, and birch tips if they could get them. If they got desperate, they would even eat jack pine tips. That same winter, in one day, my uncle Alton found sixteen deer that had died from starvation. That winter I found a total of twelve that had died of starvation.

I first saw a fawn doe that was extremely thin eating the birch tips from trees I had felled for firewood. When she first saw me, she was scared. However, I started deliberately cutting nice tender birch tips for her. She fed on them. I would bring back cedar boughs and hazel brush tips as well. Pretty soon she started following me around like a dog. I would pet her, get water for her to drink, and feed her cooked venison, cooked wheat, and pancakes. She would chomp it right down. Whatever I ate, she ate. She would follow me down to the water hole on the river when I got water and then come back up with me. I would leave a big pile of birch and hazel brush tips for her when I went trapping for three or four days. I put hay outside of the cabin for her to bed down on, which she did. The dogs never bothered her. They didn't chase her or anything. They knew she belonged there.

I always kept the snow shoveled away from the front of the doghouse doors. One time, when I came back after being gone trapping for three days, she came out of one of the doghouses. She had seen the dogs going in and out of the doghouses. So when the dogs were gone, she would go into the doghouses and sleep there. When we came back from trapping, she would come out of one of the doghouses to greet us and then go back to sleeping on the bed of hay outside of the cabin. She never slept in the doghouses when the dogs were there. She only slept there when we were out trapping. She made good company, as I was alone trapping most of that winter.

As spring approached, I had been feeding her so well that she was nice and round and fat. I began thinking, "Boy, she would be good eating." Of course, I didn't seriously entertain the idea. I had nursed her back to health and saved her life that winter. When spring approached and she could find her own food, she stopped sleeping in the doghouses or outside of the cabin on the hay bed. She came and left more frequently until one day, she never returned. I saw her at a distance once after the snow had gone down, but she never came back. She was eating green grass. She wasn't afraid of me. She just never came back to the cabin. But she was nice and fat when she left.

Packing It Out—1952

Living in as remote an area as we did, the only method of transporting anything was to pack it out. As a child, my pack-sack was a burlap gunnysack. It cut through my shoulders, and I had to put mitts under the straps. When I was twelve or thirteen years old, my dad bought packsacks for us. I could pack one hundred pounds at sixteen. By the time I was twenty, I could carry three-hundred-plus pounds for a mile.

My dad said he never saw anyone as small as I was pack that much for that long and not put it down. At twenty-four I weighed 130 to 140 pounds, and after trapping all day, I could pack 190 pounds of beaver out across the lake for two miles.

Sweet-Talking a Moose—1952

In April of 1952, I was involved in another situation in which I was in a corner. While canoeing down the Pipestone River, I inadvertently cornered a moose out on the end of a point. The ice floes and the current were driving me into the point. As a result that moose was on the defensive. His ears were laid back, his nostrils flared out, and the hair was up on his back. I knew he was going to charge, and I worried that he might jump into the canoe. If he did, he would have flipped me over into the ice-cold water, and I might not have survived.

I was carrying an older twelve-gauge single-shot shotgun loaded with number two Imperials. I started back paddling. And as I did, I started talking to him. We were only about fifteen feet apart. I just kept talking to him, all the while paddling. Easing past him, I reached for the shotgun, turning the canoe so that if he charged, I could get a shot off quickly. I didn't want to shoot him, but if he charged, I would have. Pretty soon his nostrils and his ears relaxed, and the hair on his back went down. It was a very close call. I know that it made the hair stand up on my head—at that time I had hair.

Once I passed him, he ran off. Then he stopped, and I talked to him a little more. He left and went around the point. When I came around, there he was feeding. He was only about seventy yards away, and he just kept feeding. He knew that I wasn't going to hurt him. It made me feel good to be able to save his life while not getting hurt myself.

I stopped and set a beaver trap with a long spring Victor number four trap. I had a drowning rock on the trap, so when a beaver got caught in the trap, he would drown and not suffer. Otherwise, he would go up on the bank and "ring off," which meant that he would shake his leg until he rang his foot off along with the trap. The moose just kept feeding while I set the trap. He didn't seem bothered a bit.

Bear Hides for Sale—1952

In 1952, Frank and I were going to snare and trap some bear because the lodges wanted bear rugs for their walls. The tourist business was just starting around the Rainy Lake area. Most of the tourists were Americans, and several resorts started up around the lakes. Between the Pipestone and Falls Rivers there was a salt lick near the water, which had trails that were beaten down to it by the deer. A great big bear came there, and my brother Frank saw where the bear had been traveling. He didn't want to snare any deer, so he fixed up a snare and set it on the bear trail. While he was doing this, he said that he felt like something was looking at him. He looked up, and there was a great big bear standing there gazing at him. The thing was only about twenty-five feet away. One jump and it would be on him. The bear was standing on his hind legs. He quickly reached for his rifle, but the bear turned and went off into the brush.

Later on I put another snare in there and got a different bear. The bear was caught around the neck, and he wouldn't stop moving as I tried to release the trap. I didn't want to shoot him in the body and ruin the hide, but he wouldn't hold his head still so I could shoot him in the head (I wonder why). He was just snapping his head back and forth furiously. Eventually I was able to shoot him right behind the ear. He was so small that the resort didn't want to hang him on the wall, so we gave the hide away.

In 1954, I shot a bear on the Pipestone River. He was much larger, so R.J. Fox Resort on Gull Boy Island near Kettle Falls bought the hide and hung it on the resort wall. Years later the resort burned down, and the bear hide went with it.

The Trap Line—1952

At the end of May or June in 1952, Frank and I were counting beaver houses on the trap line for the government. That was how we were able to get large quotas for beaver trapping. We were sleeping in the cabin. To keep the mosquitoes at bay in the dense woods, we put hay in a three-gallon galvanized steel water pail. We put wood in the pail and built a fire in the pail. The smoke from the fire created a smudge, keeping the mosquitoes at bay. We then opened the door to let the smoke out. There was a gallon can of lard we got from one of the lumber camps sitting outside the cabin. I woke up in the middle of the night and was half awake. I was trying to speak, but like in a bad dream I was not able to squeak out a sound. I watched in a daze as a big bear tried to enter through the cabin doorway. I finally stuttered that there was a bear coming in the cabin. The bear took off. It was just breaking daylight.

Frank didn't believe me. He thought I was dreaming until we went outside and saw the big bite taken out of the lard bucket. Sure enough, the gallon pail had a huge piece missing. That was the same summer that the bears were crawling up the trees and eating the armyworms off the leaves. Right in front of us, one of them broke through the branches and fell out of the tree onto the ground. He ran off.

We were sixteen days out counting beaver houses and didn't have much food. We had no sugar but some tea. One day, we didn't have a tea pail with us, so we cooked it up in a frying pan. We had no bread and ate only whatever we could find to kill and eat. We found some partridge eggs and robbed the nest as well as some eggs from a duck nest. They were good eating. We also shot some mallards. We were very cautious not to shoot female ducks, as we knew they were either laying or sitting on eggs. We built a fire right out on the rocks. I still remember traveling through that country barefoot to the east end of the Rat River. By the time we were done, we had something like 160 beaver houses counted. We only needed 125 houses for a quota per year of 325 beaver. We had about twenty or so houses that we did not count that were pairs, but we marked them because we knew they would have a colony the next year. That was when we found out that Lindgren Lake didn't flow into the Marsh Creek like the map was marked. It flowed into Little Long Lake, Bull Moose, Captain Tom's, and then to Little Eva and into Namakan River which flows into Namakan Lake.

Birch Lake was flowing toward Fredrickson Lake (which we called Pine Island Lake) on the map, but there was no creek there at all. It flowed into Tear Drop River, which flowed into the Pipestone. The map had it flowing the other way, west. So we wrote to the government in Ottawa and Toronto, and they corrected it on the maps. There were lakes not marked on the map that we marked and vice versa.

Always Carry a Gun—1953

Frank and I were on Pipe Lake. We were looking around for some lumber from an abandoned lumber camp, which had been a satellite of John Stewart's Lumber Camp. Frank went over to the camp by himself, and as he rounded the corner, he came face to face with a big bear, which ended up being one of five big bears that were rummaging around trying to find leftover food in the cook shack. Some of them were under the cook shack trying to get some of the leftover food residue sitting in the kitchen drain. Frank didn't have a gun with him as he had left it in the canoe. He hollered at the bears, and they took off running. One of them nearly ran over Frank on his way out. Frank did have an axe with him, but that wouldn't have been much defense against five monstrous bears, each weighing five or six hundred pounds. When he came back, Frank was just shaking. He told me the story.

I asked him "Why didn't you have your gun with you?"

He said, "I left it in the canoe. I didn't think I would need it."

My response was, "Always carry a gun with you."

We never went back to see if the bears had returned. We decided that we didn't need the lumber that bad.

The Marsh Cabin Bear—1953

Frank and I went up to Crescent Lake (Mohan Lake on the map) to build a cabin. After we crossed the Big Marsh, there weren't many deer past the Marsh Cabin. So we were living off duck. It was October or November, and everything was freezing up. A big bear had come out of his den and broke into the Marsh Cabin. I had barricaded the door shut with logs using ten-inch spikes. The big bear had pulled the spikes out and got into the cabin. He grabbed the log crossways with his teeth and just pulled it right out. You could see where he had grabbed it.

He went up on the roof first and tried to get through up there. It was roofed with sheets of asphalt. He tore the asphalt paper off the roof but couldn't get a hold of the log poles to pull them up and get inside. So he went down below and got in through the door we had barricaded.

He made a mess of the cabin. In fact, he took the dipping pail and the tin cups and our enamel plates and chewed them up. We found a jar of venison he hadn't gotten into and pulled together enough food to make a meal. After staying overnight there, we continued on home to the Falls River place.

I went back up there later to fix the roof and the cabin. I was twenty-one and wasn't happy about having to go up there alone. I had the Arisaka with me. During the two days I was up there repairing the cabin, I slept with the gun right next to me. Before we left the following spring, I set four snares, one on each corner of the cabin. He came back to the cabin in the fall of the following year and got caught in one of those snares. With the snare on and an eight-foot toggle, he climbed one of the jack pine trees on the hill and chewed all of the limbs off of it. He came back down and went almost across the river, where he died. He didn't make it all the way across the rapids. When we came back in September, we saw that the wolves were eating him. Frank and I hauled him out of there because he smelled. He had probably died the month prior. For the next three years, we had no more bear trouble.

The Cross Lake Bear—1953

We built a cabin on an island on Steward Lake, which we called Cross Lake because it had a cross-like shape. It was a good quarter of a mile from all four sides of the lake to the island. So we did not anticipate bear being there. Wes canoed up there carrying a 32-20 Marlin. Orrah Jr. had left some beaver carcasses up there to feed the dogs. However, he wasn't able to get back up there, so he told Wes to dispose of the carcasses.

When Wes came in sight of the cabin, he saw a big bear eating a leftover beaver carcass. The bear could smell the decaying beaver carcasses from the shoreline. He had crossed ice floes and swam through icy water to get from the shoreline out to the island to get at those beaver carcasses.

The bear had his back to Wes, who was still out in the lake in the canoe about twenty-five yards from the bear. He took aim and hit him twice in the rear end before the bear had a chance to move. When he did take off, he took off so fast he threw moss right into Wes's canoe. Then the bear got in the water, and Wes emptied the 32-20 into him. Wes took after him in the canoe. As the bear got up onto the shoreline, Wes loaded the .22 long rifle and hit him twice more with those shells. Wes said he went across those ice floes, through the water, and up a steep hill like he hadn't even been hit. The bear kept heading north, moving fast. Wes was worried about a wounded bear showing up at the Marsh Cabin, which was just north of that location about three miles.

Both Frank and I made several circles trying to find that bear, but it was a vast country with beautiful big open jack pine ridges, so it would be easy to lose an animal. We never did find him, but we knew that he had died because we could smell the decaying carcass.

Do Animals have Citizenship?—1954

In 1954, I was guiding at Namakan Narrows Lodge. There were bear coming to their dump, which was about three hundred yards from the lodge. The bear were coming into the yard, too. Mel Drew, the lodge owner, asked me to get rid of them, as they were a danger to the guests. I borrowed a .32 Special from Betty Berger Lessard. Betty was a guide, trapper, bush pilot with her own plane, mink farm owner, and operator of Berger's Trading Post and Cabins on Namakan Lake. I asked her how it shot. She said, "Put the sights full in the notch. You will hit right where you aim."

I went down to the dump just at dusk. I sneaked around, as I wasn't sure how many bear were there. There was a one-and-a-half-year-old cub with its mother. I shot and wounded the cub. I was on top of a hill and downwind of the old female. She came running up that hill straight at me, and I shot her in the lungs and heart. She fell twenty feet from me. I dressed out the female and hung her up. Later we would brine the bear, make bacon, and get other cuts of meat, including roasts.

At daylight, barefoot, I went after the one I wounded. When I spotted it, its ears were straight up and still. So I thought, '*I have never shot a dead animal.*' I continued to sneak up to it and discovered it had just died. It was still warm. I dressed it out and brought it home. We brined them both, smoked them, and made bacon. I had killed them on the American side but brought both whole dead bears back to the Falls River on the Canadian side for processing. Back then there wasn't much on the border in the way of officials, so citizens of both countries crossed it frequently without adhering to regulations.

On another occasion, while at Namakan Narrows Lodge, Mel Drew said, "Look at that big bear swimming across the narrows!"

The bear was swimming toward the resort dump. I responded, "Look at that moose swimming from the Canadian side to the Minnesota side!" Both animals were swimming across the narrows from the Canadian side to the Minnesota side at the same time. I jumped into our boat and turned the moose back to the Canadian side. I wanted to make sure that he stayed on the Canadian side, where I hunted and guided.

I was asked one time, "What is the difference between Canadian and American fish?" I told them, "The Canadian fish swim backward!" Actually, all fish can swim forward or backward, but most folks don't know that.

1954 – Floyd, bare footed, is pictured on the right side with the mother and cub he shot at Namakan Narrows Lodge using the .32 Special he borrowed from Betty Berger. Roy Carlson, a repeat guest at Namakan Narrows Lodge, is pictured on the left. He wanted his picture taken with the bear.

The Poplar Cabin Bear—1954

Another time, on the Pipestone River at the Poplar Cabin, we had a bear coming around. I didn't want him wrecking the cabin. I could always tell when a bear was around because our dog Sandy would start to growl. Then a whippoorwill would sound. I don't know why.

Trapping season had started in October and ended on the 15th of May. Following that, we had fifteen days of grace to bring the pelts in. It was the spring of the year, and the leaves were starting to come out. Orrah Jr., Wes, Frank and I were bringing everything in from the trapping grounds.

This bear was a menace. He was always causing trouble. You could tell he was sneaking around. The dog would growl, the whippoorwill would sound, and I would jump up and look around, and then he would be gone. I set a bear trap for him. He wasn't a big bear. He was only about 250 pounds, but he would have destroyed the Poplar Cabin. He was skinny. Usually they weren't that skinny. This was why he was hanging around trying to find food.

Sure enough, we had been gone about a day or so, and when we came back, he was in the trap, all tangled up in some crabapple bushes, which were about two or three inches in diameter. He had dug a big hole. He was mad, snapping his jaws and making an awful racket, realizing that he had been caught. Frank asked if he could shoot him with my German 7.63 Mauser. I said,

"No, I will shoot him with the rifle." That bear was real mad and was swinging his head back and forth. I shot him between the eyes, and of course it killed him.

The bear was along the river because he was eating high bush cranberries, grubs, ants, bugs, and whatever he could find, but especially thorn bush apples.

I know that along the riverbank the rough grouse were really fat, almost as fat as ducks. That was the only place in the country where I had seen real fat rough grouse (partridge). They stayed fat way up until January, and then they ate the birch and poplar tips until the end of March, when everything started greening up again for them. That was the only place in the world that I knew of, at that time, where the birds were so fat and healthy. It was a great thing to see. There were so many partridge that there were at least one hundred in a tree at a time. We shot a lot of partridge to eat as we had been eating venison all winter. We ate everything that was not damaged by the bullets, excluding the head, legs, and wings. We would even pick the feathers off and take them home for mother to use in making pillows.

Miracle at Lunch Ground Rapids—1954

On the twelfth of May 1954, it was warm out. There was green grass on the ground, and we'd already begun cutting the grass over at the homestead, and yet we *still* had a huge snowstorm. Thirty-six inches of snow fell on the banks of the Pipestone River. I left home at 7:00 a.m. to take the canoe on its maiden voyage up to the Marsh Lake Cabin, fourteen miles away, to meet Frank. I left the homestead at seven that morning and arrived at the cabin at nine o'clock that night. Two inches of snow had fallen by the time I reached the cabin.

On the way I checked traps and picked up eighteen beaver and forty or fifty muskrats. I skinned nine of the eighteen beaver on the riverbank, as well as most of the muskrats. Some of the muskrats I skinned in the canoe. It takes about nine minutes to skin a medium-sized beaver and approximately fifteen minutes to skin a large beaver. A dried beaver blanket is measured from the tip of the nose to the end of the hide just before the tail and then across the beaver pelt horizontally. It constitutes a beaver blanket when both measurements add up to sixty-five inches. Anything smaller than that is considered a beaver pelt.

I used a homemade knife made from a Swede saw file. The handle was fashioned from a deer antler. We oil tempered the saw's file so it wouldn't get brittle. I also had a Marble's Woodcraft knife. My dad had found that knife still in the sheath on Thomas

Beach on Rainy Lake just beyond Pawn Net Bay, and he gave it to me.

It started raining around noon, and eventually it turned to snow. My knees and hands were swollen from paddling my canoe twelve miles upstream in a four-mile-an-hour current, plus hauling the fully loaded canoe over seven portages. I had to paddle barehanded because mittens or gloves wouldn't have allowed me the flexibility I needed.

When I arrived at the cabin, Frank let me in. He said, "I saved half the goose for you."

I said, "What would you have done if the game warden came in?"

He said, "See that old ninety-seven Winchester shotgun? I would have said, "Have you ever eaten illegal goose before? If you haven't, start now! And besides, it wasn't illegal; I accidentally caught it in a number four-fifteen bear trap set for beaver."

Frank had about fifty muskrats. We stayed the next day and skinned the beaver and muskrats. By the following day, it had snowed another two feet. On the fourth day, we thought we should go up and complete our journey. We went up to Pipe Lake and Mohan Lake to tend some more traps.

We decided to go back to the home place. The home place was located at the Falls River, about fourteen miles from the Marsh Cabin.

Frank told me he saw a big bear up there. He said it made our dog Brownie look like a puppy, and Brownie was about one hundred pounds.

We pushed through along the edge of Marsh Lake through heavy slushy snow and ice. There was at least ten feet of snow on it. There were huge ice islands all the way out to Rainy Lake about fourteen miles away.

During that five-day period, we couldn't get to the muskrat or the few beaver traps we had up on a five-mile stretch of the Big Marsh because the snow was packed so deep.

As the Marsh widened, the current weakened and couldn't push the snowpack down the river. It was packed ten feet deep in some parts of the river.

When we got to the Marsh Cabin, the snow was three feet deep on the riverbank. We had quite a time poling our canoes up onto the riverbank because it was so dangerous. The river was much higher from the melting of the heavy wet spring snow. We had seven portages and fourteen miles to get back to the homestead from the Marsh Cabin. Going upstream we had to portage many of these, but going home we could run some of the rapids.

We stopped at a high rapid about forty feet across with a big ledge on it. Frank, the daredevil, took his canoe and pushed it out and over the portage. It slid downhill and hit the water with a big spray. I was a little scared and worried and did not want to try that. It was a treacherous situation. I got out and walked the canoe down the bank to the water, a harder but much safer method. I pulled, held, and hauled that fully loaded canoe over the bank and lowered it into the water.

We stopped at the Poplar Cabin for lunch. When we pulled in, I told him, "Whatever you do, make sure you tie up your canoe. If you just leave it pulled up on shore, the current will take it out."

After lunch, we left the Poplar Cabin. Frank followed along behind me in his canoe, and a little farther down the river, we came to the Middle Rapids, just above what we used to call Lunch Ground Rapids on the Pipestone River. There were many other rapids, but this one rapid was a big, deep, high rapid with about a four-foot drop. It had a backlash with about two feet of white water rolling back, concealed by smooth water above. We stopped there to portage over it. We pulled both canoes up on the bank. He helped me slide mine over the snow. However, he didn't tie his up. When we got back to slide his canoe over the portage, it was ten feet out into the water and going downstream heading for the rapids. Frank started to make a dive for it when I grabbed him and pulled him back. I told him, "No, don't! That will cost you your life."

My .22 bolt-action rifle was in that canoe, along with traps and about a hundred muskrats and fifty beaver. A lot of money would have been lost if the canoe sunk. The canoe turned crossways in that big rapid, and Frank said, "What should we do?"

I said, "We will sit down and pray." So we sat down and prayed.

I had seen miracles before then, but this one remains vivid and clear. The canoe turned around nose first and went straight down the rapids without a speck of water going inside of it. We jumped in the other canoe, went down the rapids, picked up the canoe with the fur in it and my gun, and paddled home.

I will never forget that situation as long as I live because it was very, very dangerous. It was not the kind of thing that a man would want to do every day.

The Pipe Lake Cabin Bear

Five days later, we came back to the Pipe Lake Cabin after the snow melted. The water was high after thirty-six inches of wet heavy snow. We had to pole down along the banks of the Big Marsh because the snow was thick in the river. The Pipe Lake Cabin was at the headwaters of the Pipestone River, between Pipe Lake and the river. There had been a big bear at the cabin. The tar pail that we had been using up on the roof to patch holes had been knocked off. I got up on the roof to see how much damage he had done. However, he had only stood on his hind legs and put his paws along the rooftop. Based on where his paw marks were on the roof, he had to be above seven feet tall. I reckoned he was about eight or nine feet long from the nose to the tail. I told Frank, "That's a big bear. He is going to ruin the cabin if we leave him."

We had just finished cleaning a bunch of fish. I had also stretched out some muskrat hides before I went to bed because they had been left for five days. After that we went to bed. Late in the night, all hell broke loose. The bear had returned. He tore down the cabin door and on his way in stepped on the dog sleeping near the door. The dog yelped, and I reached for my German 7.63 Mauser pistol. At that point, I realized that my hand and arm were asleep right up to my shoulder. So I let out a big war whoop of a yell, and the bear jumped back out of the cabin.

I knew he was going to come back. He did not come back for two days, but when he did, I snared him by the paw. We had another two inches of fresh snow. When he got caught by the paw, he turned the eight-foot spruce toggle crossways, and it looked like he had taken a bulldozer and bulldozed over the tag alders in a swath all around the snare. Tag alders are a form of willow tree, but they grow with a curvature rather than straight. Some of the tag alders were two inches in diameter, and he had mowed them over like they were grass. He got tangled up and was cutting the snare off with his teeth when we came upon him. I shot him in the nose with the pistol, which stunned him. He went to the ground. Frank jumped up in the air, shouting "Save your ammunition!" He wanted to make sure that we expended no bullets in glancing shots.

Then he shot him in the side of the head. And to make sure he was dead, he stuck the gun barrel in the side of his neck and pulled the trigger.

We cut the paws off the bear and took them home because we knew the family would not believe us. My dad brought the paws down to a Chinese restaurant in Fort Frances where they made bear paw soup out of them.

That was the end of that one, although it was kind of a hairy situation for a while because he was a huge animal weighing between six and seven hundred pounds before he was dressed out. We took thirty pounds of meat off of the underside of his hind leg, which was the most tender meat. We threw the rest of him into the river. No other animal would eat him, not even the ravens or seagulls. We asked dad why, and he said, "Because he was king of the country for many years, and the other animals are afraid of him even in death." He had only been out of the den for a couple of weeks because there was a swath of fur missing from across his chest, where his leg and paw had lain while he was sleeping in his den. It just wore off from his breathing the whole time he was denned up. He was nothing to be fooling around or messing with. It was quite exciting at the time, but I wouldn't want to do it again, unless I really had to.

The Last Deer Hunt on the
Pipestone—1955

At the end of October that year, Frank and I were at the Poplar Cabin about seven miles from the homestead. That last year we hunted at the homestead, I shot twelve deer and Frank shot seven. Between Frank, Allen, Wes, Orrah, and I, we killed thirty-seven deer that year. I had already shot a deer, so we had meat to eat. We left the deer with the family and took one of the hind legs with us to the Poplar Cabin.

Frank at sixteen years old carrying out an undressed deer that he shot near the Big Marsh Cabin.

Frank asked if he could go hunt while I was setting traps. When I got back to the Poplar Cabin, he still wasn't home. He came back that evening, and his hands were all swollen up because he hadn't taken mitts with him. When he came back, I told him, "Now I'm going hunting."

I was teasing him and said, "And I am going to get him right next to the cabin."

He said, "Go ahead; I'm going to tend the beaver sets on Clear Water Creek." Clear Water Creek flowed into the Pipestone and never froze up in the winter. So, I went out, and not a half hour later, I jumped (surprised) a deer. He ran off. I circled in on him. He went to the right, and I went to the left a little bit so I would be behind him. Then I saw a log with no snow on it. I realized that I might be looking at the deer. I had never shot anything without knowing for sure what it was. Then I saw his nose sticking out, and his horns, so I aimed right behind the shoulder, but I shot high and nicked the blood vessel on the top of his back. He got up, but he was dying. I felt bad, so I shot him square between his eyes, and the horns collapsed inward. Without thinking, I said aloud, "Oh, no! I lost the horns!"

The next day Frank shot a fawn and killed it, inadvertently wounding the doe standing behind it. He didn't know he had shot the doe until he found the blood trail. He chased the doe, and it jumped in the river. He brought the canoe over and went up and down the river but couldn't find it.

When Frank came back, he asked me where I thought it went. I said, "That doe was trying to shake you. She went back in on the same side of the river she came out on. She will go back to get her fawn."

We got in the canoe the next day, paddled up the river to the first rapids, and there was the blood trail of the deer Frank had shot on the same side of the river where it had got out. I told him to keep his gun loaded all the time. It was a 38-55 Winchester carbine, and it took five shots. I told him to push more shells into the magazine while he was running, chasing, and shooting, so he wouldn't have an empty gun when he needed it. But I knew he would unload it shooting up the woods and the gun would be empty by the time he got to the deer because that was just the way he shot. So I told him to keep spare shells in his pocket and keep it loaded. I told him that the deer would be forced over to the other side of the river.

So he chased it, and it was running. Sure enough, it jumped into the river, got out on the other side, and stopped to look at Frank. Frank took aim, and the gun went "click" because he hadn't kept it loaded like I told him. So we got back in the canoe, went up the river, got out of the canoe, followed the deer track, and the deer jumped up fifteen feet in front of me. I shot.

I shouted, "I got her! I got her!" But I was laughing so hard trying to beat Frank to the deer that I had only shot the hair off her back.

Frank said, "No, you didn't! No, you didn't!" and shot her right behind the right front shoulder, killing her. I was laughing so hard teasing Frank and trying to beat him to his deer that I couldn't have shot it anyway.

I told Frank, "I got her anyway!"

Frank said, "How do you figure that?"

I said, "I shot all the hair off her back. She would have frozen to death this winter, anyway!" That deer was one of the two fattest deer I ever saw. It was 250 pounds and had four inches of fat on it. There were a lot of acorn nuts, hazelnuts, and wintergreen on the ridges of the Pipestone. When you opened a deer up, it smelled like wintergreen.

A buck Floyd shot hanging outside of the Poplar Cabin. Floyd shot this buck with a 30/03 British Ross 30 caliber with a bolt action and a straight pull. While driving his dog team he saw the deer, slipped out the gun, knelt down, and killed him with one shot through the heart. The poles next to the deer were used to barricade the inside of the door against renegade bear.

We hung the deer up outside of the Poplar Cabin under an old tent, along with the fork horn and the eight-point buck. We canoed up another seven miles to the Marsh Cabin to set beaver traps. However, everything froze up. So I walked back down to the Poplar Cabin. Frank stayed at the Marsh Cabin. On my way back down to the Poplar Cabin, as it was getting dark, I could see tracks in the snow.

I said, "Oh, I see my dad has been here." But the closer I got to the Poplar Cabin, the more they looked like bear tracks. I got my light out, shined it, and I saw bear tracks. I was worried that he had gone to the Poplar Cabin and got the deer we had hung there. He had gone northwest and broken ice on the river, swimming across about a quarter of a mile from the cabin. He dug up the deer guts and everything I had buried, including the liver. He ate it all. It was from the deer that I had shot near the cabin. That deer was hung up next to the Poplar Cabin under the tent. After the bear had eaten up the deer insides, he was real happy. His tracks were literally bounding out of there and showed great big jumps.

The next day, I shot two deer; one was a doe, and one was a big buck fawn nearly as big as the doe. Frank came back down from the Marsh Cabin with another deer. Between that deer and the deer we had hanging at the Poplar Cabin, we had six deer. We left two deer hanging at the Poplar Cabin and brought four down in the canoe with us. It was around the tenth of November. We had a whole load of fur as well. As we were going down the Pipestone River, Frank said, "Give me the gun! Give me the gun!"

I didn't know what he needed it for, but I knew that there was a sense of urgency, so I pulled the 38-55 Winchester out of the canoe next to me and handed it to Frank. The next thing I knew, Frank raised the gun up, worked the lever, and shot a deer off the bank right between its eyes. The deer literally slid down the bank into the canoe. The bullet went right through his head, came down his neck and opened up the whole back. It didn't hurt any of the meat as the bullet went just along the top of the back. Frank said that the way the deer was running, he knew that something was chasing it, as it was running out to the river to escape. We had five deer in the canoe when we arrived back at the homestead and two still hanging back at the Poplar Cabin. I went back up after Christmas with the dog team to get the other two deer. While I was up there, I shot another eight-point buck. I came back with the three deer on the toboggan. That was the last deer hunting season we had on the Pipestone River.

Surviving Spring Breakup—1956

Frank and I went up to the Marsh Cabin by dog team on the seventh of April 1956, to start trapping. We were going to follow the ice down, as it always thaws out upstream, from the top of the river down. By the seventh of April, things were already starting to break up, but then we got a big snowstorm. Four feet of snow fell. It came out of the northeast but switched around to the south. However, it didn't thaw anything out. It stayed cold for a while, as the wind had switched back from the north. This was unexpected because on the way up to the cabin, there was hardly any snow, only a few patches on the ground. In fact, we picked low bush cranberries, which were growing out of the swamp, and made jam out of them. We cooked them down with dried apples, raisins, and about a pound of brown sugar per gallon. It made a beautiful jam. Frank and I each took a gallon with us.

We usually left one of the deer, which we had killed during the latter part of the prior fall hunting season, up at the Marsh Cabin specifically to live off during the spring thaw. It would remain frozen all winter long, so refrigeration was not a concern.

Frank and I split the deer in half around the fifteenth of April. I stayed at the Marsh Cabin and Frank went to the Pipe Lake Cabin. We trapped both sides of the river simultaneously while waiting for the spring thaw to break up the ice on the river. During breakup the ice is too thin to walk on, and the melted ice plugs the river so it can't be traversed by boat or canoe. You can't get across or down the river either on foot or by boat.

We lived off the frozen deer until the ice melted enough to get downriver by canoe. All the creeks were flooded. You couldn't go anywhere because the river wasn't open below or above. You still couldn't travel. The mounds of slush and soft ice were a hundred feet across, some of them more. There was five feet of slushy and unreliable snow and ice on the rivers. The woods had three or four feet of snow in them. So we thought we would wait the spring out.

I hadn't seen anyone for nineteen days. I worried that Frank wasn't alive. I was trying to catch another beaver because my half of the deer was depleting. It was a lonely situation not seeing each other, or anyone else, for that matter. But you had to survive. I only had six to eight stick matches, and I had to make them last. So I built a big fire outside and kept a cover over it and a big bed of logs around it. I kept it burning all the time. I split four matches in half and made eight fires with four matches. They were the traditional Red Owl matches. You wouldn't dare do it today because the starting ends on the matches are not as big, and most of them are safety matches, which means you can't strike them easily. You used to be able to strike the old stick matches on a rock. You can't do that with the matches they make today.

About a week before I saw him, I finally heard Frank shoot. I knew that it was he because of the sound of the old ninety-seven shotgun. He went down to the edge of the river and shot his rifle. Then I shot mine, so we knew that the other was alive.

About a week later, Frank finally poled his canoe the seven miles down along the side of the Big Marsh to me. He had quite a difficult time getting through the snow, slush, and ice. When I got together with Frank, I still had matches left because I had kept a fire going all the time. Frank had deboned his half of the deer and put it in gallon containers and buried it in the ground because the ground was still cold. Frank had also shot about a dozen ducks to eat. He said that he ate the meat, and the dog he had with him, Brownie, ate the bones. He had also gotten a beaver by that time.

By then the river started thawing out. We stayed there two more days and then went home. The home place was fourteen treacherous miles away.

I learned a lot of things from my mother and dad. Dad had learned a lot from the Indians along the Nelson River. He had spent ten years with them between the ages of sixteen and twenty-six years. One of the things I learned from Dad was how to survive on your own in the woods: things like how to build a fire in adverse conditions; based on the weather conditions, when to travel and when not to; how to provide your own first aid; and how to live off the land.

Wes, Floyd, and Frank with two does and a buck shot on the Canadian Kettle River. Floyd has the buck.

Practicing Beaver Conservation

Our trap line was sixteen miles long and twelve miles wide, covering one hundred ninety-two square miles, which was the reason we needed so many cabins on these lakes. We would take nine hundred muskrats a season from the Big Marsh, Marsh Creek, Beaver House Creek, Greer Lake, Falls Lake, and Cross Lake, which is Steward Lake on the map. There were muskrat houses along all of those lakes.

There were four or five beaver dams, too, which we never touched because they dammed up the waterways so that we could canoe easily. We didn't bother the beaver above the falls on Cross Lake Creek except to weed them out occasionally to prevent overpopulation. Allowing the beaver to continue to exist and dam up the lakes meant that we had good navigation all the way up to Steward Lake. Otherwise, we would have to pull the canoes over long distances of downed timber. The beaver had a dam on Steward Lake that created a twenty-seven-foot-high falls, which was absolutely gorgeous. It poured right down over the rocks.

Dad and Orrah Jr. were able to canoe up to Steward Lake, where they built a cabin on an island in the middle of the lake, largely to prevent bear problems. Like the rest of the cabins, it was used when trapping beaver.

Uncle Alton, a Man of His Word

My uncle Alton was my father's half-brother. My grandfather, Frank Paul Kielczewski I, had remarried when his first wife, Elnora, died in childbirth. His second wife was of German descent. They had three children together, first Alton and then Allen and Paul.

Alton was the second most honest person I knew, after my dad. He never told a lie, and he always shot straight. I told uncle Alton that I would meet him on a specific day at two in the afternoon at McKenzie Point. He had a mink trap around the corner, and we also had mink traps near there. It was November and the water was still open, but it was freezing on the canoe gunwales. The water was very rough, with waves almost eight feet high. Frank and I had to paddle about three miles from the homestead.

Uncle Alton had a big stretch of open water to come through in a homemade wooden boat with a five-horsepower Johnson outboard. We didn't think he would come because the weather was so bad. The wind was blowing about twenty-five to thirty miles an hour down the entire length of the lake and had kicked up some big waves.

Alton was bringing bluefin fish to bait the mink traps. I couldn't believe it when I heard the faint hum of a motor, and pretty soon Alton came around the corner through breakers that were seven to eight feet high.

"I didn't think you would come in that aged wooden boat with the little motor," I said.

He answered that he'd given me his word, and then he added, "Besides, I came in a boat, and you came in a canoe."

"Yes," I said, "But I didn't have to come across big water."

Today I would never take that risk.

Generosity of Uncle Alton

When our daughters, Marlette and Sherry, were young, we had a fourteen-foot Richline open boat with an outboard motor. Uncle Alton didn't say much, but the next time we were in Fort Frances, he took me down to the marina. He bought us a sixteen-foot covered Starcraft boat with a twenty-five-horsepower long shaft Johnson motor. It had a big deep well in the back so no waves would come in. Alton paid $2,300 for it. We insisted that we pay him back. He told us, "Okay! But pay me what you can and only when you can." Over time we paid him the entire amount.

Uncle Alton also bought me my first snowmobile. Up until this time, I had either trapped by snowshoe or by dog team. Alton flew up and got me so that I could see the one he had, which was a long ski Bombardier snowmobile. He bought me a short ski Bombardier. It was the second one that came off the assembly line in Valcourt, Quebec. After three years of random payments, Alton charged me twelve dollars interest on the eight hundred dollars. He was never worried about money. He had plenty. He was single all his life, and he had made a lot of money trapping and commercial fishing. Among other investments, he owned half of CFOB radio station out of Fort Frances, Ontario. He had also invested in a resort on Crow Lake near Nestor Falls, Ontario. As he grew older, he told me that in his later years the only reason he trapped was to have a hobby.

Marlette on the short ski Bombardier snowmobile in front of the Pine Island Lake Cabin (Harnett Lake on the map), which was formerly John Stewart's logging camp office.

A Lifetime of Guiding, Trapping, Fishing, and Hunting

I became a licensed hunting and fishing guide in Ontario when I was fifteen years old. I started by helping my uncle Allen guide on Rainy Lake during the summer months. I guided every summer from the time I was fifteen until I was thirty-two.

It was a natural lifestyle for me because it gave me the opportunity to use my wilderness skills. It allowed me to be gainfully employed while sharing the wilderness with people who also enjoyed it.

Eventually I took a job guiding tourists at Namakan Narrows Lodge on the American side of Namakan Lake. I ran Lady and Hay Rapids initially by canoe and later with an open boat. My unique ability to run both Lady and Hay Rapids on the Namakan River allowed me to take guests up the river to fish as far as High Falls. This meant that I was constantly working seven days a week from May fifteenth to October first. My days were filled with tourists eager to experience the thrill of a lifetime riding in an open sixteen-foot Larson boat powered only by a twenty-five-horsepower Johnson motor. We went up the rapids, caught our limit of fish, enjoyed some of those freshly caught fish at a shore lunch, and even took some fish back to the resort.

High Falls is one of the most beautiful places on earth. Fishing there is incredible. There is a nice spot along the shoreline just across from the falls where you can cook your catch. It is one of my favorite places.

The top of High Falls on the Namakan River.

I cooked one hundred shore lunches the summer of 1957. I put in around 140 days on the water because I started guiding in April and finished in the last part of November. I used only a twenty-five-horsepower Johnson outboard motor to run the rapids, as it was the only motor that would not catch air in the rolling waves causing it to lose both power and control. In the winters, I guided moose and deer hunters at lodges in Northern Ontario, including Eddie's Island Camp on Sanford Lake, fifty miles straight north of Atikokan. Additionally, I trapped fur-bearing animals all winter long. I guided at Namakan Narrows Lodge every summer from 1954 until 1964, when I went to the Summer Educational Camp in Orr, Minnesota.

Floyd cooking shore lunch on the bank at the bottom of High Falls.

Eddie's Island Camp on Sanford Lake was a fly-in fishing resort.

The last year I guided as an Ontario licensed guide was 1964. December of 1964 was the last moose hunt, in which I guided Bob Cary and his daughter out of Eddie's Island Camp. That moose hunt became an article in the December 1965 *Outdoor Life* magazine. I was featured in "Holiday Moose Hunt." The Ontario government wanted to promote moose hunting in Ontario, so they asked Eddie to recommend the best guide in Ontario for this hunt. Eddie chose me. Because of that article, I received many letters to take hunters moose hunting. However, I had to tell them that I was no longer guiding because in the interim we had moved to Minnesota, and I was working at the Summer Education Program (SEP) aka, 'the Camp.'

On to British Columbia—1956

For as long as I could remember, my dad had always talked of moving out to the Yukon Territory. In August of 1956, my dad sold the trap line that I owned half of. Before that, in May of 1956, Bob Moore flew up with a sixty-five-horsepower PA-11 Cub to the Falls River homestead. Dad told me that Mel Drew, of Namakan Narrows Lodge, had called Bob Moore to fly up and ask me to guide some guests fishing. Among them was Mike Taylor from Chicago, who I had guided previously. Dad wanted me to move along with the rest of the family out to British Columbia, which was to be the first stop on their way to the Yukon. I contemplated whether to stay in Ontario to guide and trap, or go with the family out to British Columbia.

After three days I decided to go and guide at Namakan Narrows Lodge. Boy, were they happy to see me! Before that, they hadn't been getting any fish, but after I arrived, we caught fish every day.

My dad was very unhappy about my decision to stay in Ontario. He came down to the resort in August to get me to sign the papers selling the trap line. Although I received none of the profit, I signed the papers. Dad was angry that I wasn't going with the family to British Columbia. The trap line was fourteen miles long and ten miles wide as the crow flies. He sold the trap line for $2,200 to Neil Cathcart. When we sold the trap line, it had nine cabins, which we had built by hand. I wished I hadn't signed the papers. My dad moved the rest of the family up to Digby Island off of Prince Rupert, British Columbia, because it was the nearest port to a railroad. They moved all the boats out by rail. Dad thought it was getting too crowded in Ontario, so he wanted to move out into the "wilderness."

They stayed on Digby Island, and I went out there from the fall of 1956 until the spring of 1957 to work at the Wahls' boatyard. Then I came back and worked at Namakan Narrows Lodge as a guide again for the summer.

I got married on September 7, 1957. Dad stayed a couple of years in Prince Rupert and then moved the family to Ketchikan, Alaska. When we went to visit Dad in 1961, he said that he wished that we had kept the grounds because he would have had something to come back to. I think he knew that he was sick. He died July 15, 1961, of a massive heart attack. He had had heart trouble for years, but he didn't admit to it or deal with it. Dad is buried in Ketchikan, Alaska.

After dad died, the rest of the family moved to Fairbanks, Alaska, and finally to Seward, Alaska.

April 1957 - Floyd's parents, Orrah Sr. and Violet, on Digby Island, British Columbia.

May 1961 – Floyd visited his family in Ketchikan, Alaska for a month. Left to right: Bill, Wes, Floyd holding Sherry, Elnora, Linda, and Mardell.

Mardell—1956

In 1956, I was guiding on the American side of Namakan Lake at Namakan Narrows Lodge where I was also staying.

Mardell was from Chisholm, Minnesota, the same town that the owners of Namakan Narrows Lodge were from. Mel and Vi Drew owned and operated Namakan Narrows Lodge in the summer months. In January of 1956, Mardell and her girlfriend, Gail Tolonen, went over to the Drews' apartment in Chisholm, Minnesota, and asked for jobs as cabin girls. Gail's older sister had worked at the resort the year before. On May 29, 1956, Mardell Swenby arrived at Namakan Narrows Lodge. I walked down to the dock to carry up her suitcases. She was staying with Martha Kaline up in the cook's quarters. I thought, '*I would never stand a chance with that beautiful girl.*'

When I met my wife I had five dollars to my name. I remember that I said, "You wouldn't want an old bushman like me with only five dollars." I remember her response: "Floyd, you won't buy love or happiness with money. It helps, but you can't buy it." I remember hearing J. Paul Getty on the radio years later saying, "I would give all my millions for one happy marriage."

I was making ten dollars a day guiding plus tips. I saved my money.

We got engaged on September 7, 1956. I left the fourteenth of October from Virginia, Minnesota, for British Columbia. The diesel train broke down in the middle of Saskatchewan, so they brought in an old steam train. As a result, I was a day late. My family had come over from Digby Island to meet the train in Prince Rupert. Because I was late, they thought that I hadn't got on the train at all, so they left.

When I got to Prince Rupert, it was three o'clock in the morning, and no one was there to meet me. So I slept in the railway station until daylight broke. Then I went down to a restaurant where you could buy a bowl of soup and a roll for eighty-five cents. When I was eating, a man came up to me, and said, "Boy, you look like an Easterner."

I said, "Yes, sir, I am."

He asked me if I had ever worked with logs before.

I said, "Yes, I have."

He offered me a job as a foreman over men putting logs into a bull chain, which took them into the mill. I couldn't believe that I had been offered a job for $2.50 an hour just that quick. I told him that I would have to get back to him because I needed to get a boat to go across to Digby Island.

I walked down along the harbor and saw a tall, thin man at Arm and Salvage Tug. Arm and Salvage Tug was a tugboat service that went out into the harbor picking up anything that broke loose from its moorings and was floating. Rich Green performed this service for the Prince Rupert Harbor area. He was ninety-seven years old when I met him and still working. Rich Green said that he had come out to British Columbia from a little town called Jasper in the Canadian Rockies on a packhorse when there were no roads or railroad. It was 750 miles by packhorse. He had crossed the McKenzie, the Athabasca, and the Frazer rivers on packhorse. Bridges cross those rivers today. I wanted to stay and hear more about his extraordinary life.

I told him that I needed to get over to Digby Island.

He asked, "Can you row a boat, young man?"

I said, "Yes, I can."

I guess he thought an Easterner wearing a suit and tie wouldn't be able to get across the "Chuck" (the ocean between the mainland and the island) to Digby Island because the ocean had a pretty hard riptide with a four-mile-per-hour current pulling you away from the shore.

He loaned me his dingy. There was no bailing can in it, so I went along the railroad tracks and found an abandoned gallon can for bailing the boat. I rowed over to the island. My family was looking out the window and commented, "Boy! That guy can really row! Look at him row!" I had a telegram that gave me directions to their house. When I walked in the door, they thought I was a ghost. They couldn't believe it. They said, "We should have realized that it was you rowing that boat!"

I went to work at Wahl's boatyard for $1.47 an hour. He owned a company that made thirty-five to fifty-foot-long fishing boats. They could build a boat a week. I worked seven days a week and sent the money back to Mardell to put in the bank. One year later, I had $1,740 in the bank. That was a lot of money in those days. I saved and scrounged. When I rode the train, I did not even pay a quarter for a pillow. Instead, I balled up my jacket and laid my head on it. I made the sandwiches that Mardell's mother had made for me for the train trip last three days. I gave my parents sixty dollars a month for groceries, although they only cost about forty. I was staying with them, so I said, "Keep it."

I rode the train back to Virginia, Minnesota, for Christmas, staying for two weeks. I then took the train back out to Prince Rupert and continued working Wahl's boatyard until the fifteenth of April, 1957. I took the train to Fort Frances, Ontario, arriving on the nineteenth of April. Mardell and her dad came and got me in Fort Frances because at that time the stretch of the train from Fort Frances, Ontario, to Duluth, Minnesota, was on strike.

Mardell and I worked at Namakan Narrows Lodge that summer. She worked as a cabin girl and waitress, and I guided.

Mardell and I were married on September 7, 1957, in Chisholm, Minnesota. Then we went up to Berger's Camp and lived in the little green, log guesthouse on the point for one year.

September 7, 1957 – Floyd and Mardell were married in Chisholm, Minnesota.

1957 – Floyd and Mardell's first home located near Betty Berger's Resort and Mink Farm.

Shot through the Heart—1957

In the fall of 1957, I was going to go deer hunting north of Thompson Beach up on Thompson Creek. I talked to Betty Berger before I left. Betty Berger Lessard was a renowned Northwoods guide, trapper, hunter, pilot, resort owner, and mink ranch operator. The house Mardell and I lived in the first year we were married was owned by Betty and located on her property on the northeast end of Namakan Lake, near the mouth of the Namakan River. She asked me where I was going to shoot the deer. Although she was referring to a geographic location, I jokingly responded, "Right through the heart." She thought that was funny and laughed.

I had the Arisaka with me, and not only did I shoot a big buck, I shot him through the heart. It was a big twelve-point buck weighing about 225 pounds. I carried it out to the Namakan River about three miles up from Betty Berger's, where I covered it up with boughs and logs so that animals wouldn't get into it right away. It was getting later in the afternoon, so I intended to come back and get it the next day. Shortly after, I saw bear tracks in the snow. It was mild out, and the bear was out of its den. I worried that it would get the deer even though I had covered it. If the wind changed, he might smell it. After having dinner with Mardell, I decided I'd go back that evening to get the deer.

We paddled back up the river. A big beaver was swimming across the river and startled Mardell by smacking its tail against the water and splashing her. Then an owl hooted loudly, ringing the timbers. Mardell jumped and said, "What was that?!" She was only seventeen and had grown up in a town, so these noises were not familiar.

Mardell and I picked up the deer, put it in the canoe, and paddled back to the cabin. Later, much to her chagrin, I showed Betty the heart with a hole shot through it. She couldn't believe it. Although I had been joking when I'd said I was going to shoot it through the heart, it became a self-fulfilling prophecy.

Early one morning, shortly after we were married, I told Mardell that I was going out to shoot a deer. She didn't hear me because she was barely awake. I left with the canoe and went over to Thompson Creek. Sure enough, I shot a nice buck. I paddled back, coming around the side of the cabin with a little seven-point buck in the canoe. It was very early in the morning. I hung the buck up on an A-framed arched "deer hanger." When Betty Berger woke up, my buck was hanging there. She was sure surprised because we had been hunting for a week and hadn't shot a deer. We had gone all the way to Kettle Falls and still hadn't got anything before I got this seven-point buck.

Bear in the Mink Cages—1957

Mardell and I spent our first year up at the Bergers' on the mouth of Namakan River. It was just after Betty Berger's husband, Bob Lessard, drowned. The Bergers wanted me to stay up there and help them with their mink ranch. I was guiding at the same time at Namakan Narrows Lodge. It was October, and Mardell and I had only been married about a month.

Betty was on a month-long trip in the Bahamas, and I promised her I'd take care of her mink, come hell or high water. One evening after dark, I went up to check on Betty's mother. On the way up, I took the ancient 38-55 rifle with me. It was two guns made into one, a Marlin barrel with a Winchester lever action. It used 255-grain bullets. I left the gun standing outside the door of her mother's log home.

I checked in on Mrs. Berger every morning and evening as she was alone and in her eighties. There was no electricity in the area at the time, so we all used kerosene and coal oil lamps or propane gas lights for light. Mrs. Berger kept a kerosene lamp by her bedside. I checked on Mrs. Berger and brought her some water. As I was leaving, I heard the mink squealing and hissing.

I turned back then, telling her, "There is more than a timber wolf in the mink cages."

I had recently broken my trigger finger at Namakan Narrows Lodge and had a cast on it. On the way down to the mink cages, I ripped the cast off. I had an awful time fitting that finger into the trigger because it was still sore and crooked, and I had a hard time moving it.

When I walked through the gate, I could smell and hear the mink. I knew something was in there, and my hair was standing on end. It was black as the ace of spades out and misting rain. I wanted to back out, but I had told Betty that I would take care of the mink for her come hell or high water.

I opened the gate to the mink cages and stepped inside. I shined the light all around and didn't see a thing. I didn't like the feeling I had. Suddenly, everything got deathly quiet. Then I saw just the hind foot of a big black bear underneath the cages. I knew then that I was in trouble. If I shot him in the foot, he would just come tearing out of there. So I waited a little bit, and then I saw him towering above the mink cages, standing on his hind legs with his back toward me. '*What a beautiful target*,' I thought. By the time I got my broken finger into the trigger, he had dropped out of sight. I had to wait for him to walk around the corner of the mink cages. In order for him to come toward me, he had to come out around the cages by the post. When he did, I took aim between his shoulder and neck, but it was dark and raining, so I couldn't see well. I fired.

The bullet went between his shoulder and neck, passed through him, and hit the chicken net behind him, leaving a big hole. When the bullet hit him, he jumped sideways, right over the top of the fence, bending it down as he went. In the next split second, a second bear was coming straight at me. I shot him in the chest. Later, I found a spiral of bear meat eight inches long on the ground where the bullet had passed through him.

I shot a second time and missed him. He leaped up over the top of the mink cages, hit the sheet metal barricade we had set up to keep out the lone wolf that had been trying to sneak into the mink cages to eat the mink food, and went up over the top of it. He hit the metal so hard that his paw prints were in the sheet metal for years afterwards. I heard them both gurgling and growling something fierce. It was an awful sound. I was holding the flashlight, the light of which was not very strong, shaking and waiting for them to come at me again. I couldn't tell where they were coming from. It was then that I realized there was not one but two bears in that mink cage. With wounded bear in the area, the darkness, and the rain, I decided not to go after them but instead took off for the cabin.

The next day I went around and caught as many mink as I could and put them back in their cages. The bears had torn open most of the cages. There were 165 mink. About 60 of them had gotten out of the cages. I found all but one, who we later found unharmed down by the lake. These mink were tame anyway. They were ranch mink and used to people. You could actually call them, and they would come up to you. I straightened up the cages as best I could, as the bears had stomped all over most of them. I went out to look for the bear the next day, but I had to go guiding, so I left before finding either of them. I never did find the bear. I think they either died or walked off the peninsula onto the mainland because they never came back.

When I told Mrs. Berger, she said, "Are you sure those weren't Ed Berger's dogs?" Ed Berger was her son, and he had two black Labradors. I said, "If those were Ed Berger's dogs, I am going to leave the country!" And she laughed.

Years later pieces of bear bone and black hair were still stuck in the post, and the galvanized sheet metal at the top of the fence still had paw prints in it.

King—1957

We had a small Border collie named King. His greatest pastime was chasing bear at the resort garbage dump. He would chase the bear, and then the bear would turn and chase him. Back and forth they would go. One time King went to the dump, and a bear had his head inside a fifty-pound lard can. King ran up, hitting the bear in the rear and tearing a large chunk of hair out of his butt. The bear rushed forward, crashing into a tree, which lodged the can on his head. He reached up with the nails on his paws to hook the can and pull it off his head. Each time that the bear nearly had the lard can off his head, King would run back up, tearing into his rear end again and taking another chunk of hair. After King had torn several hunks of hair out of the bear's rear, the bear finally got the can off of his head. He turned around and took after King, who realized that it was time to head for home. I had been watching these shenanigans from the woods. Once the bear got the can off his head, I jumped farther back in the woods. I had no weapon with me at the time.

King ran off down the road with his ears pinned back, going like a tornado. He ran right past me, and so did the bear. Neither one of them knew I was there. King ran toward the lodge and right up to the door of the trading post with the bear on his heels. The bear would not follow him up on the trading porch deck, so King escaped, again. The bear turned around and headed back for the dump. He was so angry that all the way back to the dump, he was snapping his jaws and snorting.

1965 – King in Orr, Minnesota.

Our Canadian Homes and Trap Lines—1958 - 1965

In May of 1958, we purchased a house in Mine Centre, Ontario, for five hundred dollars. It was thirty by forty feet on an acre of land and was built of standing cedar logs. It had a hardwood floor, three bedrooms, a kitchen, and a living room. My father-in-law and mother-in-law, Orton and Janette Swenby, came to Mine Centre during the summer to help us fix it up. Both Mardell and I worked at Namakan Narrows Lodge during the summer. We moved into the house in Mine Centre in September, after the guiding season was over. We had the house until the spring of 1963, when we sold it and moved up to Crilly, Ontario.

Floyd and Mardell's Mine Centre home.

November 1958 – Near Mine Centre. Floyd is hauling out an undressed deer he shot with the 1903 30/06. His dog, King, is to the right.

The Crilly General Store was owned and operated by Floyd and Mardell Kielczewski. It was the only store, post office, and telephone within 50 miles. Their residence sat behind the store.

Although the homes were our primary residences, we also lived in various trapping cabins along the trap line during the trapping season. After my dad sold our trap line in 1956, and Frank returned from British Columbia in 1959, Frank and I bought a trap line together. It was called the Harris Lake trap line. We trapped this trap line during the winter months until May of 1960 when Frank drowned up on Harris Lake. After Frank's death, I sold the Harris Lake trap line and bought another one closer to Mine Centre.

Frank and Floyd cooking lake trout they caught outside of their cabin on Mister Lake on the Harris Lake trap line. Frank's shirt is torn on his right shoulder from hauling canoes over portages.

King at the Mister Lake Cabin on the Harris Lake trap line. This cabin was built by Axle Connickson.

157

1959 - The Straw Lake Cabin was located north of the Straw Lake Mine (a gold mine on Straw Lake) north of the Upper Manitous. This cabin was on the Harris Lake trap line purchased by Floyd and Frank.

1959 - Floyd at the Straw Lake Cabin located on the Harris Lake trap line.

1955 - Floyd trapping beaver by snowshoe on the east end of Fredrickson Lake on the Kielczewski trap line. Behind Floyd and to the left is a large beaver house covered in snow.

During the summer months, we lived at or in the vicinity of Namakan Narrows Lodge, where I guided fishermen in Canada. One summer we actually lived in a tent on the Canadian shoreline opposite the lodge to avoid issues with the laws surrounding Canadian citizens living and working on the American side.

1958 - Floyd and his father-in-law at the Namakan Narrows Lodge dock unloading a 50-gallon drum of fuel oil weighing 300 pounds.

159

Early 1960s – Floyd during the period of time he guided for Namakan Narrows Lodge on Namakan Lake, Minnesota.

We left Crilly the summer of 1965 to go to work at the Summer Educational Program (SEP) in Orr, Minnesota. Originally we only intended to work for seven weeks that summer to help them plot the canoe routes. We came for one summer and stayed for thirty-five years.

Y.O.U./S.E.P. Camp Entrance.

160

Are Cabins Nutritious?—1958

While we finished our first house in Mine Centre, we moved all of our furniture out of the log cabin we were staying in at the Bergers' into a summer cabin at Shoal Lake belonging to the Cones. Lud Mehele and Lloyd Rolston helped me move our household items to the cabin.

We were only going to stay overnight. I had cooked Spam and bacon for dinner. Later that night I heard a bear sniffing around.

I said, "I hear a bear sneaking around here. I am pretty sure of it."

Lud Mehele told me, "Ah, you don't hear any bear around here."

About that time, the bear clamped his jaws around the corner of the building and took out a big chunk. It shook the whole building. Then the bear bit the corner of the cabin right next to where Lud Mehele had his head. Both Lud and Lloyd jumped out of their bunk beds. I was still up.

Lud shouted, "What was that?!"

I said, "That was the bear."

Lloyd said, "He shook the whole cabin!" It was late in the summer, near fall. The bear was looking for food to fatten up before he denned up for the winter.

Then the bear tried one more time to get at the food inside the cabin taking a second large bite and tearing another chunk out of the corner of the cabin.

I went out with a razor-sharp double-bitted axe and chased the bear off. He ran with great big leaps of fifteen feet each. His tracks indicated that he was between five hundred and six hundred pounds. Fortunately, he did not come back. Lud Mehele, however, was so shaken up that he never came back to visit either. The bear had taken two big chunks out of the building. His teeth marks remained in the corner of the cabin for years.

October to May Grocery Shopping—1958

In 1958, when Mardell and I were first married, we were living up at Bergers' Resort on Namakan Lake. In order to buy groceries, we had to go to Fort Frances by boat. When we arrived in Fort Frances, we went to Bernardi's Grocery Store. Olive (Langford) Ventura worked there. Mardell had never shopped for more than a week at a time, so shopping for the period of time from October until May was a daunting task. Olive helped. During freeze-up, you couldn't get out to town to get groceries, and after the ice froze, it was too difficult to haul any amount of food over the ice. As a result, every fall, everyone who lived back in the woods stocked food for up to seven months.

Mardell was an American and wasn't familiar with some of the Canadian names for things. She bought a case of cake mixes and wanted powdered sugar for frosting. Olive told her that what she wanted was icing sugar because powdered sugar in Canada was fine sugar.

Mardell asked for napkins, and Olive said that what she wanted was serviettes. Napkins were baby diapers. Mardell ordered a case of each spice on the shelf. This was a little over-kill, as fifty-five years later we still have some of those unopened spice cans.

We bought a case of eggs, which lasted the winter. We kept them in the porch wrapped in a feather robe. Since the porch was not heated, keeping the eggs in the robe ensured that they were cold enough but never froze. They were so cold that they were always on the verge of freezing, which was what kept them fresh.

When we finished shopping, our bill was four hundred dollars. Bernardi's gave us a fifty-pound can of sealed whole powdered milk with the large order. We never did use all of that milk. We ended up giving some of it away.

While we had to take this much food up to the lake because we would not get back out during the winter months, we also always bought enough food to share with others who lived on the lake year-round.

The Guiding Life—1958

I had guided from the time I was fifteen. Regulations stated that you had to be sixteen. I wanted to guide so bad that I lied about my age.

In 1958, I was guiding six people for seven to ten days at a time up at High Falls on the Namakan River in Ontario. We were catching trophy-sized fish. I got one northern that was ten pounds and another that was twenty-four pounds.

During this period, I guided Jim Kimball, who was the head of the Department of Natural Resources for the State of Minnesota at that time. I had the opportunity to take him up to Wolseley Lake in the Quetico Park. We were a group of five and left around 7:30 in the morning. We fished until noon and got our limit of walleyes. We went up through Lady and Hay Rapids and portaged around High Falls.

The head of the Boundary Waters Canoe Area was also with the party. At the time I did not know Jim Kimball's position. When he introduced himself, he said, "Call me Jim." A Canadian government Beaver airplane flew low over us, and I wondered why. When Art Crowfer waved at me, I realized that it was a Canadian Department of Lands and Forests (DLF) airplane (Art Crowfer was a DLF pilot). The Ontario and Minnesota governments work closely, and both sides knew where we were that day.

When the day finished, I made the comment, "Tomorrow when Mr. Kimball comes, I'll have to be on my toes."

Jim said, "You have seen all of Mr. Kimball that you will see, as I am he." He told me to keep doing what I was doing and be myself.

A couple years later, I guided Jim Kimball again. He wanted to ride up Hay Rapids, but I wouldn't let him because Mel Drew had made a decree that no guest would be allowed to ride up Hay Rapids due to the danger. But he begged me to let him ride down the rapids, so I did. He said it was better than a Disney ride.

After we moved to Orr, Minnesota to work at the camp, I continued to guide. Since I was working at the camp, most of the clients I guided were affiliated with the church.

Floyd and executives from the Y.O.U./S.E.P. Camp on Eye Lake near Kenora, Ontario.

166

1986 – Floyd on Lost Lake with freshly caught walleye.

1986 – Dr. Kermit Nelson on the same day on Lost Lake with freshly caught walleye.

167

1970s – Floyd running Lady Rapids with Y.O.U./S.E.P. staff.

Early 1970s – Floyd fishing on Wolsely Lake, Ontario.

Early 1970s – Floyd on Wolsely Lake with freshly caught walleye.

In 1973, I got my white water license. My boss sent me up to Sudbury, Ontario, along with thirteen other people from camp.

We had three days of hands-on training on the French River. They had one headwater rapids they used for training. To pass the class, we had to demonstrate ability as well as take a written test. Of the fourteen of us, only four people passed, including me. For the first time in the history of the course, the instructor waived the written test just for me, as I had no formal education.

He said, "That man there has more in his head than we can put on paper." Just for fun, I had gone down the rapids standing on the gunwales of the canoe in my bare feet.

Over the years I worked with many of the local game wardens. I was on predator control for both the State of Minnesota and the federal government. Tom Fink, Bob Kangas, Jim Akers, Ed Calise, and Troy Fonde were game wardens I worked with on predator control.

I have been trapping since I was eleven years old, and I continue to trap today.

I am also registered in the Boone and Crockett Club in 1953 for a typical white-tailed deer kill.

While I was at camp, we hunted moose every fall from 1971 to 1982. While some hunters flew over the area first and spotted the moose from the air, we did not use this technique for any of the forty moose we took out of there. We started at White Otter Lake, fifty miles straight north of Atikokan, Ontario. We either hauled everything in by truck to Clearwater West Lake and portaged it over to White Otter Lake or drove the two and a half hours on a wagon-wheel-rutted dirt road to Ann Bay on White Otter Lake. Then we would put everything into a boat and haul it out to pitch camp on an island in Ann Bay or near the castle on the northwest end of the lake.

Jimmy McQuat built the castle on the northwest end of the lake, but he was called Jimmy Hightop locally because he singlehandedly built a lone three-story castle out of red pine logs. White Otter Castle is an elaborate log building with a turret going up an additional floor. Jimmy built the castle for a woman in Scotland whom he wanted to marry. However, she never came over. He started the castle in 1903 and completed it in 1914. He drowned while netting fish in 1918. The castle still stands today and is a historic landmark.

Buck Fever—1958

In 1958, I carried a big buck weighing 285 pounds out of Straw Lake about a mile and half to the Straw Lake Cabin. After hanging ten days, he weighed 276 pounds. The rack was nineteen points, with ten on one side and nine on the other. They were mostly "typical" points, which would have made Boone and Crockett. My ankles swelled upcoming downhill to the cabin with him on my back. No wonder I recently had to have surgery on my shoulders!

Ray Camron was flying for Rainy Lake Airways out of Fort Frances, Ontario, and he flew up to pick up the deer. I sold the deer to a man I guided out of Chicago, Illinois, for fifty dollars. Ray Camron had flown John Doe* in to the Straw Lake Cabin so that I could guide him. When he missed his deer, he bought mine. Ray was going to have to fly the deer out. When he found out how large the deer was, he said, "You better fly an eight-passenger Norseman in to pick up this deer because anything smaller won't get off the lake."

They had an awful time trying to get that deer into the Norseman. He was going to tie it to the float, but he ended up having to put it inside the plane. The next summer, neighbors of John Doe's came up and said, "Boy! That was a beautiful deer that John shot." I just said, "Yeah." What I didn't tell them was that John Doe's gun misfired, and he didn't get his deer. He bought mine.

---

* John Doe is not the hunter's real name.

1959 - Floyd with the 285-pound buck he shot near Straw Lake. This is the deer he sold to a client for $50.00.

Young Walter Caribou

In the early 1960s, I was guiding for Namakan Narrows Lodge. The greatest number of people I could take up to Wolseley Lake in Quetico Park, thirty-two miles away by boat, was four. We had a party of six, one of whom had a thirty-pound cast on his leg. Mel Drew, the owner of Namakan Narrows Lodge, told me to find another reputable guide so we could take two boats. I knew the senior Walter Caribou was a good Native Canadian guide who had guided for many years. Old Water Caribou couldn't make it, so I hired his son, Young Walter Caribou. He was twenty-three years old at the time.

We started out from Namakan Narrows Lodge early in the morning heading for Wolseley Lake. We had two sixteen-foot Larson boats. One had a twenty-five-horsepower Evinrude motor, and the other had a thirty-five-horsepower Johnson motor. We had two spare motors for trolling. Both were Johnsons. One was a 2.5-horsepower and one was a 3-horsepower motor. We had four people in each boat along with fishing gear and lunch. We had to run Lady and Hay Rapids on our way up as well as portaging High Falls and Wolseley Dam.

Clients Floyd guided out of Namakan Narrows Lodge. Bill Tarrowart is pictured as the first person to the left a few years before he broke his leg.

Both Walter Caribou and I ran Lady Rapids with everyone in the boats because the rapids were straight and smaller. But when we came to Hay Rapids, due to the severity of the rapids, I insisted that the fishing party get out of the boats and walk across the portage, which is three-quarters of a mile long.

The fishing party stood on the portage at the foot of Hay Rapids and argued with me about allowing Bill Tarrowart, the man with the thirty-pound cast, to go up Hay Rapids in Walter Caribou's boat. They said, "Oh, he came over Lady Rapids easier then you did."

I said, "I know he did. I loaded his boat for him. I know what I did wrong. When Walter gets to the middle of Hay Rapids, he won't know what's wrong."

Seven people argued with me, including Bill Tarrowart, who was standing on the portage on crutches.

I said, "Hold it right now! Two years' experience as a guide doesn't give him the skills he needs to take a man with a thirty-pound cast on his leg over Hay Rapids for the first time." Every time I ran Hay Rapids, I analyzed each drop of it before I ran it. The fishing party started backing off their stance. So I put Bill in my boat with the Evinrude motor. I took some of the gear out of Walter's boat and put it in mine. I told Walter that he could follow me but it wasn't advisable because the water changed positions quickly. It crisscrossed and boiled. Walter confidently said that he could follow me.

The middle drop of the rapids had an eight-foot hole. I had to watch what I was doing, so I couldn't motion to Walter to stay to the left and then cut back right afterward. All of a sudden, I saw Bill Tarrowart's face turn as white as a ghost. He started to scream. I looked back to see Walter's boat flip over and turn upside down. I can still see the thirty-five-horsepower prop spinning around and around up in the air with the boat upside down in boiling water.

I hollered at Bill Tarrowart to stay where he was. I just screamed at him, "Stay right where you are, or we will all be in the same place!"

I turned my boat around on a dime, spinning back down the rapids. I thought we had lost Young Walter Caribou because I couldn't see him. Then I saw him pop up about sixty feet from where the boat had flipped over. He had been underwater until that point. I swung the boat over and reached into the water, grabbing Walter by the top of his gray Coast Guard life jacket. Using only one arm, I grabbed him out of the water and flung him into the bottom of the boat while keeping one hand on the motor handle and navigating the swirling rapids. With Bill and Walter in the boat, I ran my boat over to Walter's upside-down boat in the middle of the rapids.

Soaking wet and throwing up water, with water coming out of his nose, Walter helped me pull the swamped boat out of the swirling rapids by the nose rope. We pulled the boat downstream into a pocket of calmer water. We continued to pull the boat over to the shoreline. Then we tied the boat up to a tree. I then headed back along the shoreline to pick up the floating life belts, paddles, oars, and even some fishing gear. We lost one 2.5-horsepower Johnson trolling motor in the rapids and about five hundred dollars' worth of the customers' fishing gear.

After we flipped over the swamped boat, I left Walter there to work on getting the motor running. I ran Bill Tarrowart over the remainder of Hay Rapids up to the rest of the party waiting for us at the top of the portage. They had no idea what had happened in Hay Rapids. When we told them, they were just shocked.

After leaving Bill with the rest of the fishing party at the top of the portage, I went back down Hay Rapids to catch up with Walter. We worked on the motor to make sure that it was running properly. I ran it around in the basin just above the last drop of Hay to make sure that it was operating without any problem. Then I took Walter up Hay Rapids and showed him how to run it and where he had gone wrong.

We ran his boat up Hay Rapids and met up with the rest of the fishing party at the top of the portage. I then ran down the portage by foot and got back into my boat. I ran my boat up Hay Rapids again and met up with the rest of the group at the top of Hay Portage.

We portaged over High Falls carrying boats, the motors, and the gear. We went onto Wolseley Lake and fished there. I asked Walter to stay with me, but he did not. He thought the walleyes were on the reefs, but I knew that they were still on the mud flats because they had just finished spawning. So at lunch he had found only one little walleye, while we had caught our limit. We ate some of the fish at lunch, so I went back out with my boat and we caught the rest of our limit. Walter insisted on going back to the reefs. When it was time to leave, I had to go and find him. We ended up having to fill out his limit too, which put us late going back.

Since I had to run both boats down Hay Rapids, this meant that I had to run back up the portage three-quarters of a mile to get the second boat and run it down the rapids as well. Additionally, at that point, I still had to take Bill Tarrowart down the rapids in the boat because he couldn't walk the three-quarters of a mile on a rugged wilderness portage on crutches.

Because I was usually ahead of time returning to Namakan Narrows Lodge, the owners, Mel and Vi Drew, were pretty upset, wondering what had happened to the eight of us. We usually got back around 2:00 p.m., when everyone had a happy hour, took a nap, and then got up for dinner. This time we didn't get back until around 6:00 p.m. The guests pulled me aside and told me that they were going to fire Walter as a guide.

After dinner I went down to see the guests at Cabin Three. I told them, "You fellers brought this on yourself. You encouraged Walter to run Hay Rapids."

They said, "Yes, we agree with you. But he did not listen to you two more times after that when you advised him not to fish on the reefs."

I believe that Walter would have been a great guide given some experience. I didn't realize how much he appreciated me saving his life until years later, when he stopped by the camp in Orr with his children. Ironically, I was up at High Falls guiding fishermen from the camp when he stopped by. He told Mardell, "I wanted my children to meet the man who saved my life out in the middle of Hay Rapids." That meant a lot to me.

Windigo—1960

In the spring of 1960, I was running on the glare ice (ice with no snow covering it) of Bad Vermilion Lake, going to the west end of the lake to cut some cedar poles for Allen to make some pond net stakes. Pond net stakes are staked into the mud at the bottom of a lake and used to fasten pond nets. The pond nets trap fish. Allen had commercial fishing rights on Bad Vermilion Lake.

A native Chippewa Canadian named Charles spotted me running across the lake. He started yelling, "Hey! You Windigo! Hey! You Windigo!" From far away he looked like an old She Bear because he was round, big, and short. He was pulling a sleigh behind him with two packsacks on it. At a distance, I couldn't see the sleigh behind him. Thinking he was a She Bear with two cubs, I didn't want to get too close to him. So I was moving pretty fast to get by him, which is why I was running.

He kept yelling, "Hey! You Windigo!" His voice was becoming frantic. Realizing that he was not a She Bear, I screamed back at him, "I am no Windigo! I am Floyd Kielczewski!" When I caught up to him, his heart was pounding.

After he calmed down, I asked him what he meant by Windigo. He said that in the spring of the year, native Canadians fell through the honeycomb ice, but the Indians thought the Windigo got them. The Windigo is an evil spirit in Indian culture.

The Pipe Lake Cabin Bears
Revisited—1960

Uncle Allen and I flew into Pipe Lake in his two-seater, single engine fixed-pitch Aeronca Champ airplane on floats. Initially it had a sixty-five-horsepower engine in it. At the time we flew, he had upgraded it to an eighty-five-horsepower engine with fuel injection bringing it to ninety-five horsepower. He flew that plane for thirty-five years. We were going moose hunting, and on the way we decided to stop and take a look at the old Pipe Lake Cabin.

The lake was so smooth it looked like glass.

Allen told me, "This is the kind of water that has killed many a good pilot because the water is so still a pilot can misjudge the surface and fly right into it." He circled around the lake and watched the shoreline. The entire time he was landing, he watched the tree line rather than the water. We landed safely, but I never forgot what he said.

We tied up on a little island on Pipe Lake, where Allen had a set up a tent for moose hunting. He also had a canoe there he had rented from Handberg's Resort on Lac La Croix. We paddled downstream to the Pipe Lake Cabin.

The cabin's roof was caved in, and the barricade that had been across the door had fallen in. One of the barricade poles had fallen inside of the cabin. The barricade poles were about four inches in diameter and six or seven feet long with ten-inch spikes in them. Claw marks were still visible from when the bear had broken in on Frank and me. You could see that in the recent past, bear had been using the cabin to sleep in. It was nice and cool in there. You could see there was a bear trail beaten from the river up to the cabin. It looked like they might have bedded down in the back of the cabin where the roof was still intact. The old bunk beds made of jack pine poles were holding the roof up.

I said, "Look at this, Allen; there are bear living in here."

Then I told him the story of the bear breaking into the cabin. As we walked up the bear path, I accidentally stepped on a barricade pole that was part of the aged collapsed barricade and was now covered by grass. When I stepped on it, it wiggled the grass surrounding it.

Between the stories and the obvious evidence of bear living in the cabin, Allen was already on the alert, so he jumped up and cocked the hammer on his 30-30.

I had to shout, "Allen, there isn't any bear! Look, it's just me wiggling the grass with this pole!"

I had to show him three times before he believed me. He kept saying, "There he is, there he is!" His heart was pounding so hard, I could literally hear it. I thought he was going to have a heart attack. When he found out there was no bear and it was only me, he was so mad, and I was laughing so hard, that he almost caught me as he chased me down to the canoe.

The Day Kennedy Was Shot

In November of 1963, we were staying at a trapping cabin up near the Crilly Dam when we heard a knock on the door. It was after dark, and it was snowing and raining. The two guys standing at the door were soaking wet and shivering as they had rowed a couple of miles in freezing rain. They had sheared a pin on their outboard motor and been forced to row their disabled boat up the Seine River looking for help. When they saw the lights on in our cabin, they rowed over to it. My wife, Mardell, had made venison soup, which we offered them, along with venison sandwiches. They were very hungry and ate everything we gave them. We lent them some clothes so that we could dry their wet clothes off near the fire.

I made a pin for them out of a nail the size of the sheared-off pin. I cut it with a hand file to make it the right length and filed it square across the ends. I also made a couple of additional pins in case they sheared any more off. They had tools with them so that they could replace the pin. They stayed about an hour and a half and dried off. I told them that they should stay overnight, but they said couldn't because they had to meet someone above the Crilly Dam near Calm Lake. We were living in a one-room log cabin with a knotty pine floor. We had curtained it off, making two bedrooms and a combined living, dining, and kitchen area. I had bought the cabin from a fellow from Flanders for $150. They commented on how nice the cabin was. We offered that in the freezing rain and snow, they would be better off spending the night in sleeping bags on our floor then to continue on that night. But they needed to meet their friend. So I helped them portage their boat over the Crilly Dam.

Before we departed, they asked me what they owed me, and I said, "Nothing. You may have to help me someday."

We found out from them that President Kennedy had been shot.

1963 – The Crilly Dam.

1963 – The Crilly Dam. Floyd's trapping cabin was located on the shore line up in the woods.

Many years later, Guy Carnes, one of the executives at camp, and I were fishing west of Harnett Lake. We parked our vehicles and walked into what we referred to as Lost Lake. Guy wasn't feeling well that day. When we walked out, we didn't come out where the truck was parked, so we left our packsacks full of fish and walked up to a tie camp, which was nearby. They were making railroad ties out of jack pine for the Canadian National Railroad. We saw a couple of guys and asked them if we could have a ride back to our packsacks. They asked us where we parked, and I told them down the road.

They said, "We will give you a ride all the way back to your truck. We saw it." When we arrived at the truck, I asked them what we owed them, and they said, "Nothing. Don't you remember in 1963 when you helped us the day Kennedy was shot?" Guy Carnes started to cry. He couldn't believe that way up there in No Man's Land we had run into people who were happy to help us because I'd helped them so many years before.

"I can't believe it, Floyd," he said.

Recreational Snowmobiling—March 1963

We heard that they were going to put a snowmobile trail through from Flanders to the mouth of the Namakan River, down Namakan Lake to Sandpoint Lake and ending at Crane Lake. At the time, we were living in the trapping cabin on Pine Island Lake, which is Harnett Lake on the map. We had called it Pine Island Lake for years due to all of the Norway Pines that used to be in the area. I went through Pine Island Lake in 1950 by dog team. There were 60 men at John Stewart's logging camp. By 1952, they were all gone. They had logged the place out. In 1951, they hauled out and launched 17,000 logs. They took them out over the ice to Partridge Crop Lake on the Seine River. The old logging office was on Burt Grey's trap line when I bought it in 1961, after selling the Harris Lake trap line that I had owned with Frank, in 1960. We were using the old logging office as a trapping cabin.

The temperature was around thirty-five degrees above with a south wind on a Sunday in March of 1963, when Tye Murphy flew into Pine Island Lake (Harnett Lake on the map) from Tip Top Lodge on Sandford Lake.

1964 – View from the trapping cabin located on Pine Island Lake (Harnett Lake on the map).

Floyd on the ice in front of the Pine Island Lake Cabin with his uncle Allen and Allen's Aeronca Champ. The Aeronca Champ had an 85 horsepower engine with fuel injection, which brought it to 95 horsepower. If you look closely, you can see "Kielczewski Bros." on the tail.

It was the early days of snowmobiling as snowmobiles had just come onto the market. The Atikokan Chamber of Commerce had sponsored a snowmobiling weekend. They had hired Ray Cole to blaze a snowmobile trail from Flanders to somewhere around Pipe Lake because they thought they could intercept Bill Wilson's trapping trails and use those to get to Crane Lake. However, what they didn't know was that Bill Wilson had trails all over the country that he used for trapping beaver. Three snowmobilers, including Ray Cole, left from Flanders on Saturday with the intent of meeting the snowmobilers coming up from Crane Lake. However, the snowmobilers who left from Crane Lake got lost on Bill Wilson's trails. Once they realized that they were lost, they managed to get back together on Frederickson Lake. Because it was already dark, they all decided to camp out on Frederickson. They got together and built a big fire using downed wood they had gathered off the shoreline. They spent the night outside, but they were ill prepared. Fortunately, it was a nice night, and the temperatures were in the thirties.

By Sunday morning, when the snowmobilers had not shown up in Flanders, the sponsors became concerned. That was when they hired Tye Murphy to try to track the lost snowmobilers from the air. Tye tracked Ray Cole's party from Flanders to our cabin on Pine Island Lake.

Ray Cole and a couple of other snowmobilers, including a salesman for Polaris, had ridden up to the cabin earlier on that Sunday morning. Ray said he knew that he was going the right direction when he ran into the snowmobile trail leading to my cabin. Ray and his group had to spend the prior night in the woods as well. They said they were glad to see the cabin the next morning.

Ray Cole and his party were enjoying coffee and breakfast with us at the cabin when Tye Murphy and the Chamber of Commerce representative landed. The Polaris salesman had been trying to sell me a machine. I already owned a short ski Bombardier.

They came into the cabin and asked Ray Cole, "Where are the rest of the snowmobilers?"

Ray responded, "I don't know. I haven't met up with them yet."

The Atikokan Chamber of Commerce fellow was hopping mad, and he exclaimed, "That is it! You will be eating spaghetti for breakfast, spaghetti for lunch, and spaghetti for dinner!" He said, "We were expecting three hundred and forty people for spaghetti dinner last night!"

March 1963 - Ray Cole and the Polaris salesman with a Polaris snowmobile on the ice in front of the Pine Island Lake Cabin.

Tye Murphy said, "Does anybody know this country?"

I said, "I do because I was born in the area, and I have traveled the length and breadth of it with a dog team." I used to have a trap line in the same area that Bill Wilson currently had one.

Tye Murphy said, "Good. Can you help me?"

I said, "Sure. Let's go up, and I will tell you where to go." I knew that if they were lost they would have gotten lost in Bill Wilson's trails, which put them in the middle of my old trap line. So I said, "Go southwest."

Sure enough, I saw the fresh snowmobile trails running all over the countryside, clearly indicating that they had been lost. Within a couple of minutes, we saw them all bunched together on Frederickson Lake around the fire they had built. Some of the snowmobiles had gotten stuck in the slush. I was glad to see that they were back together and no one had got lost in the woods.

After we landed, they asked me if they could go on up to Pine Island Lake to meet the rest of the group. I told them, "There is no trail between here and there. It is a good ten to fifteen miles through the woods in five feet of snow." I saw that their snowmobiles were quite heavy, and I knew they would never make it through that depth of snow without a packed trail. I also knew that although it was a nice day, the weather was changing, and it was going to become bitterly cold.

I said, "No. You need to go back. You will never make it. Even if you got to Pine Island Lake, it would still be another ten miles to Flanders."

Largely they were underdressed. I just shuddered. One girl was wearing a pair of black tights.

They took my advice and turned around. They all made it back to Crane Lake safely. It was good thing they went back because that night it went to thirty-five below.

When snowmobiles first came out, everyone thought they could just go out and whip through the wilderness. The first snowmobiles were heavy, cumbersome, and slow.

Despite the fact that the Atikokan Chamber of Commerce representative was not happy with my advice, Tye Murphy said, "You did the right thing."

The next year, in January of 1965, the Ontario Provincial Police (OPP) contacted me and asked me to cut a snowmobile trail through the woods from Pine Island Lake (Harnett Lake on the map) to Little Eva Lake. George Scott picked up the trail from Little Eva Lake and cut it the rest of the way down through Namakan Lake, Sandpoint Lake, and Crane Lake.

It took me ten days in thirty-below weather during the day and down to forty-five below at night to cut the trail from Pine Island Lake to Little Eva Lake. I would run out in the morning to cut the trail and then return to the cabin at night. I had no light on the snowmobile, so I had to use the light of the moon to return home. I was so far out in the woods, and it was so bitterly cold, that it was better to leave the snowmobile running all day long rather than turning it off and risking it not starting again. So I left it running all day. At night I drove the snowmobile right into the cabin to keep it warm. It was hard to start otherwise. I had to use a handheld propane torch to warm up the crank case. It was cold starting, but it ran good once it was running.

I always carried everything with me in the event that I either broke down or had to spend the night outdoors. I carried spare snowmobile parts, a toolbox, dry socks, a chain saw, an axe, a little food, a compass, a map of the area (although I didn't need it because I knew the area), and matches to start a fire. I cut five hundred trees, made directional signs, marked all of the lakes, and posted open water warning signs in places where the ice was thin. I worked long days and into the night by myself out in no man's land and made only two hundred dollars for the ten days' work. It wasn't worth it. I would have made more trapping, but the OPP had asked me to do it, and I didn't want to refuse them.

Once the entire trail was completed, I started on my way back. I was coming from Little Eva Lake on my way home to Crilly, Ontario. I met George Scott and another fellow who had already gone to Atikokan on the trail. They were coming back. I met them on Frederickson Lake. It was two o'clock in the afternoon. Crilly was another twenty-five or thirty miles from Frederickson Lake. They stopped and asked me if I wanted some candy bars for the ride home. They offered me four of them, but I jokingly said, "No. I never steal from a man out in the woods." I only took two of the candy bars. The weather was nice that afternoon. I said, "I know this old machine will make it home tonight. I have the bugs ironed out of it. But I don't know if you will."

I made it back to Crilly just as the sun was going down. George Scott called me the next evening. He said, "You were right, Floyd. We never made it home." There were pins on the older-model Johnson machines, and one of them came out. This caused the track to break. On their other machine, the carburetor went out. Both incidents occurred at about the same time. They had to stay overnight outside on Little Eva Lake. The temperature dropped to thirty below. They walked out the next day to Betty Berger's resort to get help.

Holiday Moose Hunt Becomes an Article in Outdoor Life Magazine

In December 1964, the Ontario government promoted moose hunting in Canada. There were not enough moose hunters, so the moose were overrunning the country. Moose hunting season was from October first to January third.

In order to promote Canadian moose hunting, the Canadian government got in touch with Eddie Kaulza to get a moose hunting guide referral. Eddie told them he had one of the best in the country. So Eddie Kaulza flew me in from Atikokan, Ontario, to Sandford Lake, Ontario.

Then Tye Murphy from the Tip Top Lodge on the north end of Sandford Lake came and got me with a 140-horsepower Super Cub airplane. We used that plane to look for the snowmobiles that we were supposed to use for the moose hunt. Gert Egers and Ralph Ellibee were snowmobiling up from Atikokan. We found them on Ann Bay coming into White Otter Lake. The snowmobiles had gotten stuck in the slush. They managed to get the machines out, but they were unusable because all the slush had frozen up in their tracks. You could not even move them. The rest of the lake was solid slush, so even if they had managed to get the frozen slush out of the tracks, they wouldn't have made it down the rest of the lake. It was thirty degrees below zero, and they were wearing leather boots. Their feet ended up freezing.

As a result of the severe frostbite, they ended up being hospitalized and lost some of their toes.

In order for Tye Murphy to be able to fly them out, I had to pack the plane runway down by walking up and down on the slush on snowshoes. The 150-horsepower Cub was only a two-seater, and he could only fly one person out at a time. Consequently, he made two trips before sundown, flying them out to the Atikokan Hospital. Before he flew them out, he flew around where Ann Bay flows out into Turtle River and counted twenty-three moose. He told me, "Floyd, I may not be able to come back and get you. You may have to stay overnight." I would have had to build a fire and stay overnight in the woods in thirty-below weather with no shelter and only the outerwear that I had on at the time. I had left Crilly, Ontario, at three o'clock in the morning, and all I'd had to eat was a cup of coffee and a doughnut. I had no other food with me.

I had to break a trail seven miles from there to Ann Bay through slush all the way, and I still had to break a trail another three miles to Sandford Lake. I pounded slush all the way and knocked at least ten pounds of freezing slush off my snowshoes with the handle of my axe. Eddie Kaluza's camp was on the south end of Sandford Lake. I got there at nine in the evening and hadn't had anything to eat or drink, including water, since the coffee and doughnut early that morning. I was so exhausted that when I tried to eat, I threw up.

The next day I tried to use Eddie's homemade snow machine, but it got stuck in the slush. I told him, "This is not going to work. We will never get back to Ann Bay where the moose are."

In 1964, snow machines were huge, clumsy, heavy pieces of equipment. It was snowing like crazy, so we stayed at Eddie's for a day. Earl Thurier flew in on a Cessna 180. He flew me and the editor of the *Minneapolis Star and Tribune*, Bob Carey, his daughter, and his wife to Little Gull Lake. We spotted a couple of moose. He landed us on Bow Lake near Little Gull. Then we hunted that area and got the moose featured in the December 1965 article called "Holiday Moose Hunt" in *Outdoor Life* magazine, written by Bob Carey. Below is the article:

"Out of the blue, we headed for Ontario and a new hunting hotspot for Christmas. Clouds of powdery snow gusted around the multicolored Christmas lights decorating the homes in Fort Williams, Ontario, as we drove through the predawn darkness. Winter had slapped an arctic blast on the area, piling the drifts knee-deep along the streets and sending the thermometer chattering to 20 below.

It had taken a cooperative cab driver and a set of battery jumper cables to get our car going again after it had sat out all night next to the Royal Edward Hotel. But now it purred steadily, the heater and defroster wide open, as the headlights shone on the Route 17 sign and a black and white distance marker reading Atikokan – 127. That was our target, a remote iron mining village on the edge of a vast wilderness reported to contain one of the heaviest concentrations of moose in North America.

The glow from the dashboard light played on the faces of my wife, Lil, and 16-year-old daughter, Barbara. I wondered what lay ahead. This spur-of-the-moment trip had brought us 650 miles from Illinois, and for a fleeting second I had a feeling of apprehension that perhaps I shouldn't have brought them into this harsh country in the dead of winter.

A few weeks earlier we'd been sitting in our living room going over some Canadian travel folders and dreaming of next summer's fishing. While thumbing idly through the Ontario fish-and-game law, I noted that the 1964 moose season there ran for three months from October 1 through January 3.

'Let's go up!' Barb yelped. 'I'll be out of school on Christmas vacation, and I've never gone on a big-game hunt.'

We laughed, but the more we kicked the idea around the more sense it made. Barb's a tall, leggy junior at Plainfield, Illinois, High School, and her chief academic interests' center around music, which she hopes to study in college. But sometimes she prefers music in the form of the whisper of mallard wings early in the dawn or the raring cackle of a ringneck rooster climbing out of a wild-grape tangle. During the previous two seasons, she had scored on ducks, pheasants, and rabbits, but she had never followed big-game trails. When the Midwest deer seasons were in full swing, she was in school and could never get away for a week in the timber. But a Christmas-vacation moose hunt? Why not?

The problem was to find out if there were any hunting camps open and, if so, what the possibility was of bagging a bull in the bitter weather of midwinter.

Two years before, we had met lean, light-haired Eddie Kaluza, the 48-year-old owner of Eddie's Island Camp on Sandford Lake, 35 air miles north of Atikokan. Eddie had been in Chicago on business at that time, and we swapped yarns about lake trout and walleye angling in northwest Ontario. But Eddie had also mentioned moose, lots of them, and had said there was little hunting pressure. Now I wondered if that woods-wise bachelor would consider taking a trio of city folk in for moose, especially if two of them were female.

I phoned him at Atikokan, and he accepted the idea with enthusiasm. 'Come on in,' he said. 'There are moose all over the place. We haven't had any hunter since the freeze-up in November, and some of the bulls are dying of loneliness.'

We sealed the bargain on the spot. I was to drive to Crystal Lodge Airways just east of Atikokan, from where bush pilot Earl Thurier would fly us to the camp. Eddie said he had a plane, too, but added that Thurier's was bigger and would be able to handle all three of us and our duffel in one trip.

The days of the Christmas season skipped past as if they were hours. Late in the afternoon on Christmas Day, we were stuffing boots, parkas, mittens, wool shirts, guns, and ammunition into the car trunk. We turned off the Christmas tree lights and began the drive out of the Chicago suburbs, up Interstate Highway 90 to Madison, and northward to Duluth and Fort William.

Day was breaking and the snow as thinning as we swung off Route 17 and onto Highway 11, which runs directly to Atikokan. An hour later, we turned into the Crystal Lodge Airways base. A cold, yellow sun peered over the rim of the pines in the southeast and glinted on the two red-and-silver bush planes that stood frosty and silent on the lake ice.

The door of the two-story lodge cracked open, and Earl Thurier poked his rugged, grinning face into the bitter air.

'Come in before you freeze to death,' he yelled. We piled out of the car, grabbed our bags, and scooted up the steps. Earl's family was just finishing breakfast. While his wife, Mary, was clearing away the dishes, Earl and his sons, Gerald, Ed, and Loren, began pulling on their boots.

'We'll get rolling just as soon as I get the ship warmed up,' Earl said. 'Eddie's out at the camp, and he's got one of the top guides—Floyd Kielczewski—for you. Floyd's been out several days checking on the moose. Plenty around. You shouldn't have any trouble scoring.'

We digested this encouraging news while we fumbled out of our city duds and into insulated underwear, canvas pants, wool socks, felt boots, and parkas. By the time we were dressed, Earl had the plane raring and most of our gear loaded. Barb hopped into the co-pilot's seat, and Lil and I climbed into the back next to the duffel. With a wave to the boys, Earl opened the throttle, broke the skis loose, and we shot down the crusted runway and into the air.

The forest flattened gradually below and became a vast map of green on white. Countless ice-bound lakes lay covered by 18 inches of snow, and occasional moose, deer, or wolf trails wound from one patch of forest to another. Fifteen miles out, we spotted two cow moose moving slowly across a small bay. At the sound of the plane, they glanced up, tossed their heads, and trotted into the timber. A short distance farther, we saw a young bull standing in a frozen marsh, the sunlight glistening on his sleek, black coat.

'Look at the size of him,' Barbara gasped, her nose pressed against the plane window.

'Much bigger ones out there,' Earl said, grinning at her excitement.

The bull had barely faded behind us when the pilot cut the power, dropped the flaps, and brought us in on the snowpacked runway that led across the frozen surface of Sandford Lake to the dock at Eddie's camp. When we were opposite the cluster of log cabins, Earl switched off the ignition, and four smiling faces appeared under the wing.

'Welcome to camp,' Eddie Kaluza said, sticking out a big paw as I slid out of the plane. Introductions were made on the move as we carried our equipment into a lakeside lodge where a fire crackled in an iron stove. We met Floyd Kielczewski, who had come in from his winter trap line just for this last-of-the-season hunt. Floyd's 32 and tough as a hickory ax handle. He lives with his wife in the tiny village of Crilly (population 22) on Canadian National Railway line between Atikokan and Fort Frances. In the spring and summer, he guides fishing parties in the Namakan Lake–Rainy Lake area, and in the fall, he squires deer and moose hunters into the bush north of the railway. His winter trap line extends from Crilly into the lakes, rivers, and marshes of the moose country. Floyd had brought along his 12-year-old brother, Billy, and Billy's friend, Gert Ehlebe, 11, from Atikokan. The boys were spending this part of their Christmas vacation at the camp doing odd jobs and hauling firewood. Eddie's Husky, Prince, stood aloof, accepting us with reserved courtesy.

Eddie looked out a frosty window and said, 'There's a good wind blowing and time to get in some hunting today. Want to go out with Floyd and scare up a moose?'

'That's what we came for,' said Barb, zipping open the case on her .270 Winchester Model 70. 'Think this will do the job?'

'Some people say the .270 is too light for a moose,' Eddie told her. 'But I've killed several of them with one. Can you shoot straight?'

'Well, I can hit a target at 150 yards,' Barb answered.

'I'll back her with this,' I promised, pulling out my 12 gauge Remington slug gun.

Eddie grunted. 'You figure to use that?'

'It does a solid job on deer,' I said, 'and that big slug ought to be heavy enough to anchor a moose.'

I prefer the .270 for big game up to the size of moose, but on this trip I decided to let Barb use the rifle while I concentrated on downing a bull with the shotgun. A check with the Ontario Department of Lands and Forests assured me that the shotgun slug was legal for all big game.

200

Floyd picked up an empty quart-sized oil can and said, 'Let's see you hit this, Bob.'

We trooped outside and he put the can on the snow 75 paces away. I held as steady as I could, sort of 'wished' the shot in, and squeezed the trigger. The can flew backward three feet, a big hole ripped through both sides. I was smart enough to quit while I was ahead, and while the effect of the shot was still fresh I handed the gun to Eddie and suggested he try a shot. Eddie slammed the can on the first try, and Floyd almost tore it in half with another shot.

'That thing shoots all right,' Eddie said, looking at the shotgun with new respect. 'Let's get some lunch, and then you can head for the bush.'

Just then, Barb came out of the cabin in her hunting outfit, and the two men doubled up with laughter. 'What have you got on your head?' Floyd howled, pointing at her long blue-and-white knit cap with a fluffy white tassel.

'That,' Barb said indignantly, 'is my ski cap. It keeps my ears warm, and don't you dare make fun of it.'

Floyd and Eddie shook their heads and started up the path toward the cabin. Though they were well-versed in the ways of moose, deer, bears, and bobcats, it was obvious that trying to understand a teenaged female was out of their element. Floyd swore it was the first time he had guided a hunter who wore two feet of knit headgear.

To get into moose territory over deep snow, Eddie used a pair of ski-equipped power sleds that had been welded together side by side and hitched to a ski-rigged wooden cart. The homemade rig was powerful enough to move a couple of moose.

After lunch, we warmed the engines and loaded up. Lil, who loves any kind of fishing but has only a fleeting interest in hunting, took some ice fishing tackle and headed for a canvas shanty that Eddie had erected on the ice 200 yards from shore. Floyd, Barb, and I hopped on the power sled and aimed for Little Gull Lake, where the guide had spotted two cows and a bull earlier.

The sun was in the 2:00 PM position when we pulled up near a timbered point in a small pothole just off Little Gull Lake.

'We go on foot from here,' Floyd announced, checking the cloud movement for wind direction. 'We're about a mile downward from where I think the moose are. We should be able to move in on them if the wind stays up. From now on, we don't talk. I'll indicate what to do by hand signals. Any kind of sound—voice, sneeze, cough—will spook them clear out of the country.'

Since we had four days to hunt, I decided to leave the shotgun in the sled so that I could handle both the black-and-white and color cameras in case we lucked into a moose and Barb got a shot. Floyd had his Model 1903 .30/06 Springfield in case Barb needed backing. Single file, we broke trail through the heavy snow along the lakeshore into a small bay, where we swung into the thick jack-pine forest.

Floyd edged along slowly, moving a dozen steps or so and then stopping to watch and listen intently. The wind sighed in the treetops and shook loose cascades of snow that came showering down around us. The forest floor was marked with odd shapes where the snow lay over stumps, rocks, and windfalls. About 200 yards from the lake, we hit a set of moose tracks that were apparently only an hour or so old. The tracks angled toward an opening in the trees ahead. We tensed as Floyd added more caution to his already careful movements.

The tracks ran up a ridge that curved back toward the lake. Floyd stopped, shook his head, and indicated silently that the wind would carry our scent to the moose. Quietly, we backtracked to the lakeshore and moved along it to a point directly downwind from the ridge. Plunging into the forest again, we worked toward the top of the slope. At the crest, we eased into a clearing where there was good visibility for 200 yards. Nothing was stirring except a raven that sailed into a thicket below.

Floyd was puzzled. He had expected the moose to be somewhere in view. We moved slowly across the ridge and looped around and doubled back, passing less than 30 yards from our original trail, and headed upwind toward a small valley. We plodded through the deep snow, often falling over buried obstacles and stopping periodically to get our breath. Two more sets of tracks joined the original trail, and all three headed into the valley.

The sun had disappeared below the timber, and the air was getting sharp. The puffs of clouds were changing to long, hazy strips that promised more snow. The woods were growing dark, and I was beginning to wonder if it was time to head back when Floyd raised a hand and cocked his head to one side. Somewhere ahead there was a rustle of branches that was out of tune with the normal motion of the trees in the wind. We stood motionless, listening and watching, for perhaps five minutes.

All three of us saw the antlers at the same time. The dim, grayish brown shapes moved erratically as the bull raised and lowered his head. In the gathering darkness, it was hard to tell which way he was facing. His body was partly obscured by a cedar sapling which he had apparently pushed over to feed on.

Floyd motioned Barbara to a spot where visibility was clearer and indicated that she was to look through the scope. Barb slipped off her mittens, raised the rifle, took a look, and lowered the gun.

'All I can see is a big, black body,' she whispered, her hands trembling a little as she stared at the swaying rack.

'Aim about two feet below and a little to the right of the antlers and let him have it,' Floyd whispered back. I got busy with the cameras, but in the gloom, it was impossible to get Barb, Floyd, and the moose together.

It's Barb's big moment. Floyd, our guide, directs shot.

203

Barb put the rifle to her shoulder and put her thumb up the stock to the safety. Floyd and I watched her intently while trying to keep an eye on the moose at the same time. Though she had taken her share of small game, this was her moment of truth in the big leagues, and we had no idea what emotional effect the moose would have on her.

More than one grown man has turned pale, got the shakes, fired into the air, or become frozen to the trigger at the sight of a bull moose. Barb was flushed and excited, but she stayed cool, took a deep breath, let out half of it, and squeezed the trigger.

The .270 roared, jerking her head with the recoil, and there was a crash of underbrush as the bull pitched forward into the cedar and out of sight. 'I got him!' Barb yelled. 'I got the moo—' But the last word stuck in her throat when the bull lurched to his feet and began moving away. He was broadside to us now, and we had a clearer view. He was black and huge. Barb's second shot plowed into his rib cage, spattering the snow with red. He skidded to his knees but got up again.

Barb was stunned. 'Give him another!' I yelled hoarsely. She worked the bolt but never got the shot off. The moose banged into a couple of saplings, and Floyd let go with his .30/.06, finishing him with a shot through the neck.

We moved up on the animal with rifles ready, but the bull was done. Barb's eyes grew as big as baseballs as she gazed at the trophy.

'Holy cow, it's so big!'

'Nice moose—900 to 1,000 pounds,' Floyd said, and he bent over to bleed the animal. Barb grabbed an antler and tried to lift the head out of the snow.

'Is that where I hit him?' she asked, pointing to the hole in the rib cage.

'That is where the second shot went,' I said.

'Where'd the first shot go?'

Floyd was inspecting the carcass. 'The first one took him high on the back leg,' he told her, 'and went the length of the body. Any one of the shots would have killed him. I put that last one in just to make sure. Couldn't tell from back there just how hard he was hit.'

Barb watches Floyd raise the head of her bull for photo.

The sky was growing darker by the minute, and small flakes of snow were drifting down. Floyd worked fast with his knife, opening the body cavity and pulling out the entrails. Then he separated the heart and liver and impaled them on branches so that we could carry then easier.

'We'll prop him on his knees,' he said, 'so that he'll cool properly and the birds won't mess up the meat. Eddie and the boys can come in tomorrow and haul him out.'

The body cavity was spread open with sticks, and we tugged the moose onto his knees. That done, we wiped the blood from our hands and picked up the rifles and the heart and liver. As we started plodding through the snow back to the lake, several ravens appeared out of the forest and, with guttural croaks, dropped in to feast on the offal.

Supper that night at the lodge was a delicious feast of buttered potatoes, green beans, and fresh, golden brown lake-trout fillets by courtesy of Lil, who had taken the trout through the ice on a small, silver plug.

During the meal, Eddie filled us in on the history of the area. Atikokan had come into existence a little over 15 years ago when a road was dynamited and bulldozed through the wilderness from Fort William to reach the rich iron deposits in the bed of Steep Rock Lake. The road made accessible a vast piece of fishing and hunting territory that formerly was touched only by fly-in parties from Fort William or Fort Frances.

But there was no rush of sportsmen to the area. The road dead-ended at Atikokan, offered no access from the west or south, and was considerably out of the way for Americans coming in from the easy but roundabout route from Duluth to Fort William. However, recognizing the recreational values as well as the importance of mining activities in the area, the Canadian government began extending the road westward to Fort Frances. The work was completed last summer, and the road now provides a shorter, more direct route for fishermen and hunters from the Midwest.

Though local hunters work close to the highway for deer and moose, the best moose territory lies 30 to 40 miles north of the road. There are a couple of rough forest trails into the area that can be used by four-wheel-drive vehicles, but up to now most hunters have gone in by outboard boat, canoe, brush plane, or powered snow sled. There are half a dozen resorts scattered over the area, and canoe outfitters and float-plane services are available. The Atikokan Chamber of Commerce is a good source of information on hunting and fishing facilities.

Eddied told us that though the new road will make the area more accessible to sportsmen, there is little danger to the fish and game populations. To the south is 2,000-square-mile Quetico Provincial Park, and to the north and west is a 1,400-square-mile wilderness area within which no resorts or permanent establishments can be built. Eddie's camp is on the edge of the latter area.

He takes care of eight to twelve anglers a week during the spring and summer, and parties of four to eight moose hunters in the fall. The November freeze-up makes it impossible to get hunters into the area by boat, but Eddie and Earl Thurier are promoting the idea of using powered sleds for late-winter shooting.

After supper, we verbally re-hunted Barb's bull and rehashed some other moose hunts of past years. Lil told about catching trout in the dark ice shanty and the fun of watching the silvery fish dart for the lure she was jigging in the clear water below.

'Looks like you're the only one who didn't get anything today,' piped Floyd's little brother Billy, as he grinned at me.

'I'll get my moose tomorrow,' I answered. But I hadn't figured on the weather.

In the morning, a wet blizzard raged in from the southwest. The air was warm, but visibility was cut to 400 yards. Though going out in a blizzard was a little risky, Floyd and I loaded our gear, including a pack of emergency supplies, and headed for White Otter Lake. He and Eddie had spotted a herd of seven moose there a few days before, and one of them was a bull which had what they figured was a near record rack.

We didn't make it to White Otter. Two miles from camp, the sled ground to a halt. The heavy snow had pressed down on the lake ice, forcing up water and forming half a foot of slush. The machine plowed into it and stalled. Floyd cut a sapling and used it as a lever to raise the machine while I cleaned the slush off the tracks, but it was no go. We stalled every 200 feet. After two hours of futile effort, we gave up and went back to camp. The next day, the snow and slush were so bad it was difficult even to walk anywhere, except on the packed plane runway.

Floyd tries to free slushed-in sled during wet blizzard.

Eddie felt bad about the situation and said he had never seen winter conditions like these. (A check with Canadian government officials affirmed that 1964 was indeed an unusual winter and that during a normal season snow-sled travel on the lakes is usually easy.)

The snow began to lift about noon on our last day, but there was no time left to hunt. Earl Thurier flew in, and the afternoon was spent cutting up Barb's moose and loading it and our gear into Earl's plane. Another snow squall was on the horizon when Lil and Barb climbed into Eddie's plane for the trip out.

From Left: Earl, Eddie, and Floyd load the rack and moose meat into plane.

Earl took me for a short flight over White Otter so that I could see the territory Floyd and I would have hunted. In an eight-mile radius from camp, we saw 35 moose, including an immense bull that rose out of his bed, shook his antlers at us, and trotted regally into the forest.

At the Crystal Lake base, we said goodbye to Eddie and Earl, packed our duffel, and put two frozen hindquarters of moose in the car trunk.

Though our trip was hurried, we found that midwinter moose hunting has some advantages. It's easier to locate and bag a moose with good tracking snow on the ground, there's little chance of losing a wounded animal, and the meat from the trophy keeps in excellent conditions. Furthermore, we didn't see another hunter the whole trip.

'It's New Year's Eve,' Barb said as we turned onto the road to Fort William. 'Let's make a resolution to come back next year and stay at least a week so that Dad can get his moose too.'

Flying Bobcat

Uncle Allen told me a story of a time in the late 50s when a trapping friend of his, Pete Basaraba, had a trap line and was trapping out of King Fish Lake. Pete was trapping for any fur-bearing animal he could get a hold of, including fox, wolves, bobcats, beaver, fisher, and mink. He was flying a little J3 Cub that he used for trapping. He landed on one of the lakes he had traps on to tend his traps. In one of his traps, he had caught a bobcat. The bobcat was still alive, so he shot it in the head.

He threw the bobcat in the little open baggage area just behind the only two seats in the plane. Then he hopped in the plane and took off. When he got up to 3,500 feet elevation, Pete had an eerie feeling that he was being watched. He glanced back to see that the bobcat had come alive and was sitting up behind him, staring at him. The bobcat was ready to pounce on him. Pete knew that in a fight with a bobcat at 3,500 feet, he would lose. With the bobcat staring at him, Pete very slowly and gingerly reached back and opened the window next to the bobcat. He made sure to move very slowly so as not to alarm the bobcat any more than he already was. When he opened the window, the wind came whistling through the plane. The bobcat, seeing a route of escape, jumped out the open window. At the same time, Pete tipped the plane so that as the bobcat flew through the air, he wouldn't hit the back wing and cause the plane to go into a spin. The bobcat went sailing through the air as Pete wondered to himself, *'Will he land on all fours?'*

Pete then realized that the bullet, which had initially hit the front of the bobcat's skull, had actually just glanced off the skull, gone over the top of his head, and come out the back, only stunning the bobcat, not killing him.

This is just one example of the many adventures encountered using small bush planes as a means of travel in the wilderness.

Can You Help Us Make a Portage?

We were telling stories one time, and Uncle Allen got to laughing so hard he had tears running down his cheeks. He was choking up so badly he could barely get the story out.

Loren Erickson had stopped by Uncle Allen's place on the Canadian side of Rat River to show him his new ten-horsepower Mercury motor. The new motor was giving him trouble. So Loren and Allen went out for a boat ride to try to fix it. Loren had the Mercury motor mounted on an open fourteen-foot Alumacraft boat. The motor would kick in and take off really fast and then almost die and then kick in again. Loren was busy trying to get the motor to work properly and not watching where he was going. So back and forth it would go, with the motor kicking in and the boat taking off in a fury, or the motor suddenly dying. While Loren was intent on fixing the motor, Allen was watching the shoreline come up pretty fast. All of a sudden, the motor kicked in and the boat hit a sand beach at full bore, cleared right out of the water, jumped through tag alders, and landed on the beach on the other side of a little peninsula on Berger Island.

While Allen and Loren were shocked to find themselves grounded on the other side of a beach, they were even more surprised by the fact that a stark naked couple was making love on the beach beside them.

The male jumped up and exclaimed, "What the hell is going on here?!"

Quick-thinking Allen sagely replied, "We are making a por-tage. When you get done there, can you help us out?" All this was going on while the motor was up in the air, still running and making an awful whining racket. Loren Erickson said he was so embarrassed. Loren and Allen quickly pushed the boat off the beach and departed in haste. There was no damage to the boat or motor because the water was pretty high, so the tag alders and little slip of beach on the peninsula were pretty narrow.

The Depression Years at Camp-
1965–1968

When we lived in Crilly, Ontario, we had a two-story home that was three times the size of the cabin in Orr. It had hardwood floors, three bedrooms, running water, central heat, and a telephone. We also owned the only grocery store, post office, and telephone within fifty miles. On our property we had another twenty-by-sixteen-foot home, which we rented. I owned my own ninety-square mile-trap line with three fully finished trapping cabins with hardwood floors.

When we came to camp (the Summer Education Program) in Orr, Minnesota, it was at the request of church leadership who wanted me to map out the canoeing routes in Northern Minnesota and Northern Ontario. We intended to go back home to Canada at the end of the summer and continue our lifestyle of trapping in the winter months and guiding during the summer. My average annual income per year in Canada was five thousand dollars, derived from guiding and trapping. When I agreed to come to camp, I was told that my annual salary would exceed that annual figure and that a fully functional home would be waiting for us to move into. Neither of these things was true.

The first summer I worked at camp, we stayed in Katera's Cabins just outside of the town of Orr, Minnesota. I had to paddle back and forth across Pelican Lake in a canoe to go to work at the camp. I worked six days a week for up to fourteen hours a day. Even though I was hired to plot canoe routes, I ended up digging ditches, constructing septic systems, and helping with camp construction.

At the end of the summer of 1965, I was asked to work for the camp on a permanent basis. However, we were only given one day to move from Canada. As a result, we sold everything in haste, leaving Canada with only our clothes. The camp was still under construction, and that first year, there was no running water and no indoor plumbing, and the cabin we were living in was not winterized. It was just a small one-bedroom one-bathroom cabin. Even though we took out the wall between two cabins to make one larger cabin, we still only had two bedrooms. We had to heat the makeshift house with a barrel stove, which we placed in the center of it. I insulated the entire cabin myself, taking the outside paneling off and insulating the walls. I scrounged up some scrap paneling, which I put around the base of the cabin to keep the pipes from freezing. I crawled under the building and insulated the floor using a staple gun. Then, when the snow fell, I banked up all around the house with snow, which provided additional insulation.

We had to wash clothes at a neighbor's home, and I had to buy the propane tanks myself for the gas stove. There is a photo of two of the girls, Mardell and me, standing outside of the camp cabin we lived in year-round looking like every bit like the grim life we were living.

Between the trapping and guiding in Canada, we had a comfortable lifestyle. However, in the early years following our move to the camp in the United States, I was only making seventy-six dollars a week.

After I came to the S.E.P. camp in 1965, I didn't have a lot except three small girls. It was pretty hard the first few years. When we lived in Canada, I had a much greater opportunity to catch fish and hunt deer and moose, which significantly reduced the grocery bill.

Floyd, Mardell, and Marlette outside the Bayview Cabin with Sherry peeking out the door of the cabin.

I couldn't get out and hunt and do what I needed to do to help the family because I was no longer self-employed. I was only clearing $134.00 every two weeks.

We had no vehicle, and we couldn't afford to buy one. So, Mardell and I would snowshoe out a mile and a quarter one way to the neighbors to pick up the groceries we ordered from the local grocery store. In the winter months, Mardell helped me shovel off sixty-five roofs to keep them from collapsing under the weight of the snowfall, even though she was not on the payroll. She was helping me shovel off roofs when she was eight months pregnant with our fourth daughter, Sarah.

In the summer of 1966, there was not enough housing on camp for all of the faculty. As a result, we were told to find our own housing because there was not enough room for us. We were forced to move out of the cabin and find our own place to live. The only place we could find in the area was a primitive cabin with no indoor plumbing. If not for Phil and Bee Christensen, we would have been living in a tent. Phil and Bee offered us their cabin, which was twelve miles from camp. It was a primitive cabin with an outdoor toilet and no running water. We had to haul water in ten-gallon cans for everything, including drinking, cooking, and washing, but we were grateful to have it. I drove back and forth to work every day in a Chevy pickup I borrowed from the camp.

We lived this way for three years, until Garner Ted Armstrong, one of the church executives, changed that by having a new house built for us on campus. In 1968, we moved into our first new construction home. The house itself was not completely finished. It was sheet rocked but not finished off. When we first moved in, there was no plumbing, and the house was sitting on top of the hole in the ground that would later be a finished basement. The most amusing part of this unfinished home was the fact that it had been moved in backward. Consequently, the kitchen door was ten feet off the ground and the front door opened into the lilac bushes. They had to hand-crank the entire house around, which took all day and a lot of swearing. We lived in that house for the next thirty-three years, until we retired in the year 2000.

This photo was taken in the last year of the thirty-three years we lived in this house on camp.

Despite a rocky start, the next thirty-three years at camp were fulfilling. Mardell and I met many great people who we are friends with yet today. I came to the camp when I was thirty-three, and my wife was twenty-five. She was sixty, and I was sixty-eight when we left. I retired on May 31, 2000.

Timber Wolves

I have never had a wolf attack me, but they have been known to attack a dog, if you had one with you. They would kill the dog. I heard several firsthand stories of people who had wolves kill their dogs out on the ice right in front of them. Because they did not have a weapon with them, there was nothing they could do about it.

I have had four experiences where a timber wolf or wolves were going to attack the dog that was with me. In the daylight, they backed off. But in the dark, I had several stalk me for three or four miles.

The first time, I was up on the north side of Namakan Lake near Thompson Creek on a little lake they called Jackfish Lake. It is on the map but not named. The Bergers called it Jackfish Lake because it had little jackfish in it. Across the lake, I thought I saw a deer following my trail down the cliff behind me. Because of the cliff, it had to zigzag down. However, I could see that the cadence it had was too smooth for a deer. It was snowing, and the snowflakes were large. The wind was in our favor. When it was about three-fourths of the way down the cliff, I realized that it was a wolf. He was purposeful in his approach, so I knew that he was not just curious. He was after the dog. My Border collie, King, was with me. I did not have a gun. All I had was a sharp chisel and an axe. I knew that he was going to grab the dog, so I

221

took off my mitts and grabbed the chisel. If the wolf attacked the dog, I intended to spear it right through its side.

The dog was barking at him. He was watching the dog intently, and I was ready for him. All of a sudden, he saw me. He turned and wheeled back. The dog took off after him. I called to King to come back, but he continued to chase the wolf. After they disappeared into the woods, I heard King yelp, and I thought, '*Oh, no. The wolf got the dog.*' However, King come running back. His hair was up on his back. I don't think the wolf bit him, but he might have nipped him. King was just a pup at the time, and ever after that, he was afraid of wolves.

Another time I was on snowshoes in February on Harris Lake, not far from the Straw Lake Cabin, which was where Mardell, Marlette, and I were staying. At the end of the day, I was headed back to the cabin.

It was already dark when I heard wolves growling and barking at me. My gun and shells were in the bottom of my packsack. They ran across the lake to the right, and then they went through the woods and across the portage to the south again. I barely got a glimpse of them. King had seen them on the lake, and he growled. I shined the light right away, got my gun out, loaded it, and kept it with me. They followed me in the dark for three miles and jumped across the trail on the portage in front of me. They leaped completely across the trail, never touching down on it. They followed along in the woods on the right side for three miles and eventually peeled off.

I thought there were no more than three of them, but when I saw the tracks the next day, I saw there were five. I didn't shoot at them, but I had the gun out and ready to go. King walked tight against my leg the entire time.

When I was coming down the railroad tracks as it was getting dark, Mardell would come out about seven in the evening and shine a flashlight toward me. It was good to see the light. The only time she did not do that, a wolf followed King and me right up to the cabin.

When I saw the tracks the next morning, I saw that he was never farther than ten to fifteen feet from me the entire time.

I did see him run across the tracks in front of me and I did see a flash of him alongside of me, but I did not have a flashlight. I did have a sharp chisel. I hollered at him, and very wily-like, he slipped away. However, he continued to follow us right up to the cabin door. The wolf was after the dog, not me.

The fourth time was the following spring when I was pulling a beaver out of a trap in the ice. King was with me. King barked a deep growling bark and came running straight toward me. A wolf was chasing behind him. King's hair was up on his back. I grabbed the .22 rifle I had with me. The wolf was about twenty-five yards away when he saw me. He then turned and wheeled back into the woods. I think there may have been more than one wolf, but the snow had already melted off the ice, and I didn't bother to track him.

Camp Bears 1965–2000

Virtually every year at camp we ended up having to kill a bear. Despite our best efforts to "bear proof" the property, they would come in and become a menace to the five hundred students and staff. Following are some of the stories.

On the seventh of September 1969, about one o'clock in the morning, we were in bed when a bear came through camp and turned over the garbage cans. I jumped up and grabbed the 38-55 lever action, which held eleven shots, that was standing by the bedroom door. Wearing only my underwear, I flew out the front door. I saw the bear and shot at him twice in the moonlight, but I wasn't sure if I had hit him. I was afraid that I might have shot a hole in our neighbor, Adolph Bjoraker's, Jetstream trailer or his Cadillac. In the moonlight I had to aim between the trailer and the Cadillac in the attempt to hit the bear. He took off, and I decided not to chase after him in my underwear.

The next morning I saw a hump on top of the Dorm Two hill. It was the dead bear. There were two bullet holes in him about four inches apart. On closer inspection, I saw that the bear had a broken front leg that had healed up crooked. He must have been looking for food in the garbage cans.

In 1965, when we first came to camp, we were staying at the north end of a duplex called Bayview. Mardell's dad was sleeping in the living room on a studio bed. I heard an awful racket outside. Our dog King was raising Cain, barking and growling.

Mardell said, "I think it is a bear."

I said, "No, it is probably a fox."

I looked outside and saw a great big bear blowing and snorting at our dog while eating King's dog food. This bear was between six hundred and seven hundred pounds. It was as long as our six-person table and just as high. Mardell's dad had been drinking beer, so Mardell told me to throw a beer can at him.

I told her, "No. The element of surprise is better."

I had no gun, so I opened the screen door, jumped out onto the porch, leaned over the rail, and hollered at him so loud you could hear the echo across the entire bay. The bear got so scared he literally flipped over backward. The bear took off down the road, and King went after him, barking up a storm. Mardell's dad jumped up and stood in the middle of the floor, hollering, "What the Sam Hill is going on here?!"

The bear knocked over small balsam trees running away. He never came back.

Three weeks later I got a telephone call from a neighbor who lived a mile and a half away. Mrs. Coyer was whispering in the phone, "I have a prowler."

I had previously borrowed a .32 Special Winchester Lever Action Model 94 rifle, which carried eight shots, from another neighbor, so I grabbed that and ran the mile and a half down our dirt road to Mrs. Coyer's. On the north side of the house, I saw big muddy paw marks on the window. He had pawed the entire length of the bay window. That's when I realized her prowler was a bear. I went in to talk to Mrs. Coyer and told her that I had found her prowler and he was a bear. She said, "Oh, no."

Later on, someone else shot the bear. I saw it at the dump. It was the same bear that had been eating King's food. There was a huge hole right through the neck. I don't know who shot him. I never saw a bear bigger than that.

In 1983, one of our camp dogs, Sandy, chased a 350-pound bear around and around. The game warden told me to go ahead and get rid of him, as he was mean. Every time I started out after him, he would take off and be gone. On one occasion, the bear was chasing Sandy, who tucked her butt up underneath her legs as she ran to keep the bear from getting her. The bear chased the dog until the dog ran underneath the porch to escape. I aimed between his eyes and took a shot. I used the Remington Gamemaster Pump. The first shot went off, but the casing did not come out. I pushed down on the extractor, and the casing came out. I managed to get the second shell in it. Fortunately, I did not have to shoot the second time, as with one shot the bear was dead. The bullet went between his eyes and came out behind his right ear. The reason the gun had jammed was because there was dirt behind the extractor. Later I took the air compressor and blew out all the dirt.

Dr. Nelson, the camp director at the time, had served vegetarian hamburgers for lunch. I was going to give our dog Peggy Sue one of the hamburgers. So I got on the moped to go find the dog. I heard her barking and followed the sound down to the shoreline. I thought that she had treed a raccoon. When I got there, I realized that she had treed a bear. She was jumping halfway up the tree trying to get at him. He was growling and snapping his jaws. I did not have a gun or anything with me. So I ran down to the house and got the .35 Remington Gamemaster. I shot at the treed bear. He was so mad that he was shaking his head back and forth, and I ended up hitting him in the jaw. I shot him a second time in the head, and he fell out of the tree and into the water near the shoreline. I dragged the bear out of the water and up onto the bank. Since I had to take people up fishing early the next morning, I had someone else from camp call the game warden to come and get the carcass. He came and disposed of the bear.

During that same period of time, we had another bear come into camp right among the kids. I had to get rid of it, so I shot it, of course. When I told the game warden, he said, "Go ahead and get rid of it. You can't have kids getting mauled on account of a bear coming into camp."

The bear would lie down in the woods behind the infirmary where there were a couple of dumpsters and watch the residents marching up to the dining hall for meals. Everyone in the camp ate all of their meals in the dining hall, and all five hundred people ate each meal within a one-hour period of time. A dorm was scheduled every five minutes. Staff and faculty ate at any time within that one-hour period.

We tried to make sure that the camp was kept clean and free of any debris and trash to prevent bears from coming into camp. We emptied the garbage cans daily and rinsed them out with chlorine. When the bears swam across the lake, they would look for a place to come out that was high and dry. There was a swamp behind the higher land on the edge of the lake. That point we called "Girls' Point" had all of the girls' dorms were on it. The bears tended to come out of the water there and travel along that point because it was much higher and drier than the swamp behind it. As a result, they frequently walked through Girls' Point and arrived at the epicenter of camp. I can't tell you how many bears I ran off, chased away and did everything I could short of shooting them. By and by, I had to shoot that one. It was a big bear weighing in at about four hundred pounds.

Mother and Cubs

In the late eighties, we were living at camp. It was late in August, and early in the morning, about 3:30 a.m., when my son-in-law, JR, called me. He said, "Floyd, there is a drunk outside!" I stepped outside of our front door and listened. What I heard was a cub bear howling, which sounded just like a drunk. But I knew it was a bear.

I grabbed the .35 Remington Gamemaster, which I kept in the bedroom, and loaded it up with shells. Then I went outside and walked over to the side of JR's house. The dogs were barking, so I hollered at them to stop. Once they stopped barking, I heard the leaves rustling on the ground and realized that the mother bear was at the base of the tree. Then I saw that she had her paws on the tree, and she was trying to get up to the cub. She was growling and snapping at the dogs. I told JR to call the dogs off and put them in the house. He did.

Then I started talking to her. The hair was up on her back, and her ears were back and flat. She was ready to fight to defend her cubs. One cub was up the tree she had her paws on, and she had put the other cub up the tree next to it. She had put the cubs up the trees to get away from the dogs. She wasn't charging, but she was snapping and growling at us. I could almost see that she was saying, "Let me get out of here with my cubs." I backed off and kept talking to her. If she was ten feet closer, I would have had to shoot her because she could have killed us in one leap.

She was mad, her jaws were snapping, and she was ready to fight. I backed off about forty yards. I had a good, powerful light, and I kept it on her. As mad as she was, there was no room for error.

She muttered something to the one cub, and down the tree the cub came, just like that. Then she went over to the other tree, muttered something, and down the tree the other cub came. She started to leave with the cubs in tow.

I hollered, "Get out of here now!"

I can still see her running down the beach, her front paws coming up behind her back legs with the cubs running behind her. She and the cubs never came back. I was so happy to be able to save her and the cubs' lives. The local game warden and I had a good relationship. When I told him the story, he gave me a hard time about getting soft. But I was glad that it worked out the way it did.

In the spring of 1958, I was over trapping in Bliss Lake north of Seine Bay. I had paddled down Bliss Lake Creek from Bliss Lake to Seine Bay in a canoe. I trapped a whole bunch of beaver, which I had skinned on a portage. I left the carcasses on the portage. Two days later, I was with Dalton Smith in the same area. I told him, "This is a good place for a bear to be." Just as we were pulling up to the portage where I had left the beaver carcasses, I heard a growl. The sun was setting and shining right in Dalton Smith's eyes. He said later that he couldn't see the bear but he could hear her growl. The hair was right up on the bear's back. The bear was only fifteen feet away, and it looked like it was going to jump in the canoe. I started back paddling right away, turning the canoe sideways so that I could shoot. I shot the bear with a 30-30 lever action rifle twice. The bullets were two inches apart.

I wondered why the bear had come so close to us. Then I heard rustling of leaves in a tree, and I saw three cubs. I felt so bad. I realized that the cubs would not survive without the mother. It was the last part of April, and those cubs had just come out of their den. They wouldn't have made it without their mother. So I shot all three of them.

Evidently, she ran the cubs up the tree when she heard us coming. But she was only ten feet from shore, and with one jump, she could have landed in the canoe. If she had been farther away or if I could have backed off another fifteen feet, I would have let her go. Or if I had known at the time that she was a sow, I would have tried to get farther away. When I shot, I thought it was a big boar bear.

Only an Axe—1965

In 1965, I was working at the summer camp and had gone up to Beaver House Camp guiding some people. Beaver House Lake is in Quetico National Park in Ontario, Canada, so no guns are allowed. It was Saturday morning, and I was alone. Everyone else had flown out in Scott Erickson's Cessna 180. I slept in the food tent that night because I knew there was a bear around, and he was likely to get into the food if I wasn't there to stop him. I was in a sleeping bag on the floor of the tent. The sun was just rising when I saw the tent start to lean in on me. I grabbed my axe and unzipped the tent door. By the time I got the tent door unzipped, all I saw were the brown pads of his disappearing feet. That bear had been only two feet from me. His pad marks were clearly stamped on the outside of the tent where he had leaned on it. The paw marks remained there even after it rained. According to the pad marks, he was a good-sized animal, around three or four hundred pounds. Nothing to mess with, and all I had was an axe to defend myself.

I was alone until Monday when another group flew in from the camp in Orr, Minnesota. I never did see the bear again. I must have scared him bad. He had smelled the food in the tent, but not me.

In 1970, Garner Ted Armstrong flew into Beaver House. The summer camp had rented a twenty-foot Grumman canoe from Handberg's Marine, which was up at the Beaver House Camp.

There were only two tents and two couples, so I slept under the canoe. I always had a tarp with me, so I covered the canoe with it. I set the tarp up so that no water would come in under the canoe, and I used moss to make a bed. The food was also stored under the canoe. Even though it rained all night, I remained warm and dry.

Garner Ted and his wife were not as fortunate. Their tent had started to leak. So early in the morning, he got out to try and dry things out.

The ranger at the ranger station located at the southwest corner of Beaver House Lake had told me that there had been bear problems on the lake. As a result, when I heard the noise, I thought it was a bear. I came out from under the canoe with my axe swinging. When Ted saw me coming out with the axe in my hand, he shouted, "I am not a bear, Floyd!"

Lightning Strikes!

I have had several encounters with lightning striking, but the closest call I ever had was in the last of part of July, 1956. I was guiding at Mel Drew's resort, Namakan Narrows Lodge, on Namakan Lake. That morning it was really thundering and lightning. I said to Mel, "I don't think I am going to go fishing today." His response was, "But, these guests are crying to go, Floyd." I said, "OK," and I got out the rain gear. Due to dithering about whether or not to go fishing that day, we got a late start. We left the dock at 11:00 am. It was still thundering and lightning when we left.

We left in a 16-foot open Larson boat with a 25-horsepower Johnson motor and a spare 3-horsepower motor for trolling. We headed up Namakan River on our way to Wolsely Lake. This was the period of time before Bill Tarrowart's near death experience in Hay Rapids when I was still allowed to take guests with me in the boat up Hay and Lady Rapids. We ran up Hay and Lady Rapids to the bottom of High Falls. We left the Larson boat tied up at the bottom of High Falls and portaged the 25 and the 3-horsepower motors over High Falls along with our cooler and ice for the fish and sandwiches for shore lunch.

It was not legal, but for convenience sake, we had stashed (hidden) a boat in the woods above High Falls on the Canadian side. In this manner, we only had to portage motors and not the heavy boat as well.

I put the 25-horsepower Johnson motor on the back of the boat. We called it a Shoe Boat because that is what it resembled. It was a 14-foot open boat with a square back and a round front. It was similar to a John Boat with only two seats running the width of it. The one seat in the middle is where the three guests sat. I sat on the seat in the back next to the outboard motor. There was probably only three feet between me and the three guests in the middle seat.

As we headed into Wolsely Lake, it was raining so heavily that I could not see, and I had to stay near the shoreline to find my way down the lake. We were about 40 feet off the shoreline traveling at 35 miles per hour when, BAM! there it was! A white ball of light came right out of the clouds through the rain and passed between me and the guests. I literally watched the lightning pass between us in a twinkling of an eye. It did not hit us, but I could feel the intensity as it passed by. The lightning slammed about five feet up a white pine tree on the shoreline. When the lightning hit the tree, it exploded in a fiery white ball. The lightning traveled through the tree and hit the ground dislodging a rock four feet across. The tree was burning, the rock cracked in pieces, and chips of the tree landed in the boat as we passed by. It all happened in a split second, but the after affect was as if a bomb had exploded. The impact was so great; it actually caused the lake to come up as if it had been hit by a meteor.

Although shaken, we carried on into Wolsely Lake and caught our limit of walleye before returning back to the resort that afternoon.

In July of 1971, Rod Wilkerson, an executive from the Y.O.U./S.E.P. Camp, and I were up at the fishing camp on White Otter Lake. We had set up a fishing camp on an island about 400 hundred yards long and 100 yards wide just southwest of the Castle. There were no campsites established on this lake, so we had to bring in or build everything we needed. We built our own outhouse by digging a hole in the ground, and made a frame for our toilet out of standing dead spruce which were two and a half inches in diameter. We made a tent out of plastic and set it up over the toilet. We had even brought up a regular toilet seat and installed that in our framed-in toilet stand.

Rod and I were cooking breakfast in the cook tent one morning when lightning hit not 30 yards from us. Rod jumped up in the air. "Too late, Rod," I said. "It has already hit." We went outside to see where it hit and found that the lightning had hit a tree, which had exploded. Even more concerning was the fact that a sliver of the tree 20-feet long and 5-inches in diameter had split off and speared into the trail going to the outhouse. One of the guys from our fishing party had just come back from there and had walked down the trail just before the lightning hit the tree. Rod said, "Boy, that could have killed someone."

In August of 1954, I was working at Namakan Narrows Lodge when the owner, Mel Drew, approached me and said that the point in the middle of Namakan Narrows was on fire. He had seen the smoke and called the Fire and Forestry Departments in Crane Lake, but he couldn't get in touch with anyone. He thought that we shouldn't let it continue to burn, and he asked me to go over and see what I could do.

When I got there, the ground was literally on fire. Apparently, lightening had struck a big white pine tree, which was 30 feet up on the hillside. When the lightning struck, it ran down the tree and trailed into its root system. There it smoldered for two days before surfacing and starting the tree and ground on fire. I took my axe and chopped up the burning stump right down to the roots. The fire was smoldering at least a foot down in the ground. Even the rocks in the ground were hot. Once the tree, stumps, and root system were chopped up, I ran up and down the 30 foot hillside carrying a three and a half gallon bucket filled with lake water to drown out the fire.

Mel Drew came over and said, "It looks like you got it out, Floyd." But the Fire Marshall from Crane Lake wanted to come up and take a look anyway. After he inspected it, he said, "We don't need a Fire Department up here...just Floyd Kielczewski!"

The upper piece of the white pine tree, which snapped off when it was hit by lightning, is still on the hillside nearly 60 years later. It is almost rotted away.

Three Deer Bagged with Two Bullets—1966

In November of 1966, during deer hunting season, I went hunting about a half a mile from camp down across the railroad tracks. I was sitting on a rock looking down underneath the balsam trees. I saw several deer legs going through the forest. There appeared to be six of them. I whistled at them. They stopped. I took aim and hit a big doe right through the neck near the shoulders. The deer went down at the crack of the gun, and I heard the other deer run. I could hear two deer run away, but the sound of one of them wasn't right. It sounded like a deer that had been wounded. It sounded like a death run. I had shot enough deer in my lifetime to recognize that. I went ahead and dressed out the big doe. After I dressed out the doe, I tracked the second deer.

I followed the deer tracks and found that the second deer had run about fifty yards and fell down. I dressed the second deer as well. I had hit two deer with one bullet as they had been standing side by side. I had shot the doe in neck, and the bullet went right through her neck and through the fawn standing behind her.

"Oh, dear," I said. "I have never done this before."

I knew Frank had shot two deer with one bullet, killing one and wounding the other, which we got later. But I had never shot two deer fatally with one shot. I followed the remaining set of deer tracks and shot a third deer, thereby firing two shots and killing three deer.

Scott Erickson was on his way to work when I came out of the woods. He stopped, and I told him that I killed three deer with two bullets. I had to tell him three times before he understood, and he said, "That's one for the books, Floyd!"

Do You Think They Heard Us?—1971

As Told by Mardell Kielczewski

From 1971 to 1982, we went moose hunting up on White Otter Lake, which is fifty miles north of Atikokan, Ontario. The road went north from Atikokan to Clearwater Lake. At Clearwater Lake, it branched off onto a wagon-wheel rut to Ann Bay on White Otter Lake. It was two and a half hours drive from Clearwater Lake to Ann Bay, which was only seven miles. You had to have a four-wheel drive and go really slow. There were huge rocks all along the primitive dirt road. During that period of time, we took out a total of forty moose. They ranged in age from calves up to twenty years old. Floyd personally drove out almost all of them.

In the fall of 1971, Floyd and I were camped on an island near Jimmy McQuat's castle.

We were going out early to go moose hunting. It was 4:00 a.m. when we got up. Floyd started whispering.

I asked, "Why are we whispering?"

Floyd said, "So the moose won't hear us."

We carefully and quietly walked down to the boat and loaded it up.

I said, "Won't they hear the boat motor running?"

Floyd said, "They are used to boats, but they will be disturbed by the sound of human voices."

We got into the boat and started down the lake to the castle on White Otter Lake. As we came around the bend, the motor started malfunctioning. It would run and suddenly cut out, start to die, and then Floyd would monkey around with it, and it would start up again. So it would go fast, then really slow, and then kick in again. Floyd was intent on fixing the motor, and I didn't want to say anything, for fear of the moose hearing me, about the fact that we were quickly coming up on an expansive white sand beach. All of a sudden, the motor kicked in, causing it to move the boat furiously forward, which drove it right up onto the beach. When we hit the beach at full throttle, I was thrown up into the bow of the boat, along with all of the guns and everything that was in the boat. It made an awful racket. The motor was up in the air roaring away. The lake echoed with the noise of the crash landing and the whining motor, which was still running in midair.

Floyd turned off the motor as I whispered from the front of the boat, "Do you think they heard us?"

Floyd shouted in frustration, "Don't be crazy, woman! Anything within fifty miles heard us!" We had been whispering for three hours.

We had to go back to camp using the alternate five-horse-power motor. We crawled back to camp, and it took Floyd five hours and forty minutes to repair the motor. We did not have the tools we needed. So Floyd had to make a Phillips screwdriver out of a flat screwdriver using a file. Floyd tempered the screwdriver in the water. When he was done with that, he broke the top off the file where it was brittle right below the soft spot to make a key for the flywheel. The flywheel had sheared the key right off. Floyd took the timing plate off using the using the Phillips screwdriver he had made. He set the points and tightened up the condenser with his thumbnail. The key he made out of the file went into the slot for the flywheel. The camp sold that motor about five years later with the homemade key still in it. The motor was still purring like a kitten.

Floyd at the moose hunting camp on White Otter Lake, Ontario.

Mardell and Floyd at the moose hunting camp on White Otter Lake, Ontario.

243

Moose Hunting–1971–1982

Early in the morning of the following day, we went out hunting again. We went back up the lake past the Castle, down the river that went to Turtle Lake. I stopped the boat just to listen. I heard a *crack!*

Mardell said, "What was that?"

I said, "That was a moose."

We heard a second *crack!* Then I knew it was a moose. So I drove the boat to the shore. Mardell stayed in the boat, and I went upland. I went into the woods about where I had heard the crack sounds. Sure enough, there were fresh moose tracks and droppings. The droppings were warm, so I knew he was close. I had on a blue nylon jacket, which made noise when I moved. So I took it off, hung it up on a branch, and started tracking the moose. I came to a little lake I thought he would be on the shore of. There was a little beaver dam on the right side of the lake. He wasn't on the shoreline, but all of a sudden, the moose coughed. It sounded almost like a man. He must have been eating and gotten something stuck in his throat. I couldn't see him.

I said to myself, "I wish he could cough again."

Sure enough, he coughed again. Then I spotted him on the other side of the lake. It was a good 250 yards across the lake. I shot five shots at him. He flinched, but he didn't fall. He just kind of disappeared.

I knew that I had hit him. So I went over to the spot where he had been standing, and I saw blood. Then I looked up. He was standing not more than thirty yards away, looking at me looking at the blood. When I saw him, he had his butt toward me, so I thought I would wait until he turned to shoot him again. But he took off straight ahead because he wasn't hurt. He had only a little cut about an inch long on his neck where a bullet had grazed him. I followed him, but he kept going and going. Finally, after tracking him for some time, it was getting late in the afternoon, so I went back to the boat. I had given up on that moose.

We went back to the camp on the island. Early the next morning, about 4:00 a.m., Mardell said, "Why don't you go back after that moose? You always said you don't want to leave a wounded animal. You would feel really bad if you found him later dead and all bloated up."

So we went back out. We went back to the same place on the shoreline. This time Mardell waited on the shoreline. I took the old 38-55 with eleven shots. I went into the woods and found his track again on bare ground (there was no snow). It was October. I found where he was feeding, and eventually I found his bed. Then I found a second bed half dry. The heat of his body had half dried out the wet bed. It had been raining all night.

I said to myself, "*I will have to kill him in his next bed.*" If he caught the scent of me or saw me before I saw him, I would lose him because he was already savvy to me.

The wind was blowing from the south in my favor. As I came up over a little ridge, the landscape looked just like a park. It was spruce swamp with no underbrush. There were a couple of turned-over roots. He was lying down behind one of the roots.

I said to myself, "Oh, look at my moose. Just like Mardell said he might be, he's dead and bloated." He was lying on his side. On the left, at the end of the root, there was about eighteen inches of his butt sticking out. On the right end of the root, I saw part of his neck and shoulders sticking out. Farther up, I recognized the nose. I wasn't sure if he was dead or alive, but I thought to myself, '*I have never shot a dead animal.*'

Then, I saw his ear flicker. I aimed right between his shoulders and pulled the trigger. He jumped up, and I hit him again in his jugular vein. Standing up, but still in his bed, he wheeled around, and I shot him on the other side of his jugular. I was only aiming at the neck and head but managed to shoot him twice in the same spot. I shot him again in the neck and once again in the head for good measure.

Sitting on the shoreline, Mardell said, "There goes Five-Shot Floyd again." Later she said, "Aren't you glad that I told you to go back out again?"

I said, "I sure am."

That moose weighed about five hundred pounds dressed out. It had an inch and a half of fat on it. It was a beautiful animal. I carried it out to the boat in two trips. The day I shot it, I dressed it out, quartered it, took the heart and liver out, and deboned the jaw (to have the teeth analyzed to determine the age). I hauled out two quarters, and Mardell hauled out the neck. I elevated the remaining two quarters to keep them from souring and then covered them with pine boughs for the night. I came back the next day to haul out the remaining two quarters. Early the following day, we left for home.

When the moose teeth were analyzed, it was determined that he was two years old.

In 1974, we were on another moose hunting trip up on White Otter Lake. This year we set up our moose hunting camp on the island just due north of the boat landing. It was a sheltered island out of the wind.

Dr. and Mrs. Lochner; their son-in-law, Dave Harris; their son, Otto Lochner; Mardell; and I were on this trip. Dave, Mardell, and I went out to the only large island on the lake, which was five miles long and two miles wide. On this island were two points with a bay in between them. Dave and Mardell were stationed behind a large rock on one point. Dr. Lochner and Otto were on the other point. I was going to drive out the moose to Dave and Mardell.

247

I heard the moose rutting, calling a cow on the north end of the island. Dave, Mardell, and Dr. Lochner were on the south end of the island. I tracked the moose down. He started moving, but the brush and timber he was in was so dense that I could only see his horns floating above the thick underbrush. I took aim and missed but hit his horn. He made an awful squeal, bounced like I had gotten him, and took off. I chased him toward the south end, but he doubled back. He must have sensed there was someone on the south end of the island as the wind was in his favor. The north end was a steep rock wall that no moose would go off of. When he came back around, I chased him back again to the south end. All in all, I ran fifteen miles around that island before I got him off. When he got into the water, he turned back and looked at me. The hair was up on his back, his ears were flat back, and he flared his nostrils and snorted and blew at me as if to say, "Go to hell, Kielczewski!" Then he swam off the island, heading toward Dave and Mardell.

Unfortunately, they started shooting prematurely while he was still in the water swimming. Mardell literally emptied her gun, shooting at the moose. In the process of shooting, the magazine screw loosened up, the cylinder holding the shells fell out, and all of the shells fell out of the gun. In the meantime, Dave was unloading his gun in the general direction of the moose. The moose turned back around and was swimming back toward me. He came fully out of the water onto the shoreline, turned broadside, and looked back at Dave. Dave had one shell left. He took time, rested his gun on the rock he was hiding behind, and shot him with one shot through his heart. For all the shots that were fired at him, he was hit by only two. There was a hole in his horn and in his heart. He made a little circle and fell down dead on the beach. This was perfect because we were able to dress him out on the beach, load the whole animal into the boat, haul him down to the boat landing, and drive him the two hundred miles back to Orr, where he was skinned and quartered.

In 1973, Dr. and Mrs. Lochner, Mardell, and I went on a moose-hunting trip. Everett Littler was supposed to come with us. He was going to hunt with us but not stay with us. He was going to stay at Ray Cole's Lodge on Clearwater West Lake. That year we were camped on the portage between White Otter Lake and Clearwater West Lake. Before we left, Everett said, "If I don't come up tonight, I'll be up there tomorrow." He did not show up that night.

The next morning I was a little concerned. I told Mardell and Mrs. Lochner, "I better go look for him." I took the eighteen-foot Crestliner, which had a twenty-five-horsepower outboard motor. I was about halfway down Clearwater West Lake when I saw the end of a wooden canoe sticking up out of the water. The first thing I thought was, '*Oh, no. He drowned.*' There were good-sized waves about four feet high, and the wind was blowing hard out of the southwest. On this lake there were no islands except one little one on the far end. The canoe was about fifty yards off the shoreline. It was standing straight up in the water with just the nose sticking out.

I followed the shoreline farther down, looking for him, and I turned around and came back down the shoreline. I did this three times. I was going to give up because I thought that he had drowned, but I went one last time. I didn't see him. So I turned and headed back to the campsite. As I did so, I looked back and saw Everett on the shoreline waving frantically at me. He was stripped down to his underwear. I wheeled back around and met him on the shoreline.

He said, "I am so glad that you came back. I thought you were going to leave me."

Earlier that morning, Everett had headed down to our campsite in his canoe. The waves were too high and the wind was too strong for the long shallow canoe. The canoe had a sawed-off back and a five-horsepower motor. When he swamped, he had the good sense to grab a gas tank and use it to help him float while he swam to shore. He said the waves were so high that he had to hold his breath as they came over him so that he wouldn't drown. When he got to the shoreline, he went deeper into the woods to get out of the wind. He had no way of building a fire because everything was lost when he swamped the canoe. He was soaking wet, so he took his clothes off to wring them out. Because it was so cold and windy, hypothermia began to set in. Due to the high winds, he did not hear the motor the first couple of times. When he did hear the motor, he was so far back into the woods he had to run some distance to get out to the shoreline. When he finally made it out, I was already heading back, and he thought he was lost. When I found him, he was already turning blue from the cold.

I took my outer layer of clothes off, my jacket, my mitts, and my boots, and gave them to him. The clothes were still warm from my body heat, and I still had my inner layer of clothes on. We went back to our campsite, where we had spare clothes. He put those on. We put him in front of a roaring fire and gave him a shot of brandy. It took him about three hours to warm up.

That afternoon, Everett, Dr. Lochner, and I went back out to find the swamped canoed. We got the canoe, brought it back to camp, and were able to dry it out. Most of his items actually floated to shore, including his packsack, so he lost very little. If I hadn't found him, he may not have made it.

As Told by Mardell Kielczewski

On November 10, 1975, I was alone at the moose hunting camp. We were staying on the same island we always stayed on, just north of the landing at the mouth of Ann Bay on White Otter Lake. Floyd, Clem Hendrickson, and Carl McNair were out hunting moose on White Otter Lake.

As evening wore on, no one had returned to camp. It was incredibly dark out with no moon or stars visible. The wind was howling out of the northwest. There was a point on the north-west side of the island that had a protected little sand beach. Behind the beach was a huge sand cliff that spilled down onto the beach. Since no one had returned, I was concerned that they might have difficulty finding their way back to the camp. It was so dark that you could not distinguish the land, the water, or the horizon. It was completely black. So I took my flashlight and went down to the beach because that faced the rest of the lake, and I knew that they had to come from that direction.

I gathered up a bunch of driftwood and built a fire. I sat there for a while as it was warm near the fire and relatively protected from the terrific wind. Probably forty-five minutes later, I heard Carl's motor nearing the beach. Carl hollered at me as he went around the island to the campsite. I went back to the site to meet Carl.

Carl said, "I was never so glad to see a fire in my life. I didn't know where I was, and I had no idea where to go. Then I saw the fire, and I thought Mardell must have built a fire."

The fire was still burning when Floyd and Clem Hendrickson came in. Floyd said it was so black that they couldn't see each other in the woods. It was so cold and windy that the entire shoreline was covered with a foot of ice. The ice was way up on the bank from the wind blowing so hard.

Floyd said, "Something drastic is going to happen in this country because this is the kind of weather that people don't survive in." That night, only 150 miles away on Lake Superior, the Edmund Fitzgerald sank, drowning all twenty-nine people aboard.

The last moose hunt on White Otter Lake was in 1982. Carl and Dottie McNair, Mardell, and I went on that trip. We pitched camp on the same little island north of the boat landing.

We went hunting in Blind Bay, the entrance to which is narrow and full of boulders. I went up onto the beach and noticed that there were what appeared to be dog tracks. I thought, '*Someone must be hunting with a dog.*'

I put Carl on a stand, and I went into the woods to drive out a moose. In the woods, I heard a *crack!* It sounded like a moose going through the woods. I heard the *crack!* again. Among burned black tree stumps, I thought I saw the legs of a moose. I kept looking and looking and pretty soon, I saw a nose sticking out around a tree. I couldn't see the shoulders because of the dense timber. I aimed for its heart and fired one shot. It bolted off. I shot a second time and missed it. I followed it, and I saw it on the downside of a hill. I shot the moose right between the eyes. I dressed it out there and covered it up.

We left Blind Bay and went to hunt on the big island. Two days later I drove a moose off the big island. Carl was waiting behind the big rock (the same big rock that Dave Harris had been hiding behind). He saw the moose swimming toward him, but it was farther down the shoreline. So Carl ran into the woods and down the shoreline, out of sight of the moose. He met the moose right where it was coming out of the water and shot it. This was the last moose we ever took off of White Otter Lake. Carl and I dressed out this moose, loaded it in the boat, and brought it back to the campsite.

That same night all four of us went back to Blind Bay to retrieve the first moose. I went back into the woods, and just as we were getting close to where I had left the covered moose, I heard a deep bark. The resounding bark sounded like a timber wolf. Thinking that a timber wolf had got to my moose, I was so angry that I raised the gun up to shoot him. When he raised his head, I could see he was a hunting dog. So I called to him, and he started wagging his tail. He hobbled toward me. His feet were all swollen, and he was pretty skinny. It was apparent that he must have gotten separated from a hunting party. He had just found the moose, and he was just starting to eat the lungs and liver of the moose.

We quartered the moose right there. The hound picked up the moose tongue to chew on it.

But, Carl said, "No, No, Buddy." We knew his name because he had a dog tag with the name "Buddy" on it. As hungry as he was, he still dropped the tongue.

When we left Blind Bay, it was dark, black as the ace of spades. We had one whole quartered moose, four people, and one dog in a fourteen-foot aluminum boat with a twenty-five-horsepower motor. We were about six inches above the waterline, but the lake was calm, so we made it back to the island, picking our way around the boulders in the narrow entrance out of Blind Bay.

When we got back to camp, we soaked bread in milk and fed the hound just a little since he had not eaten in so long. His feet were so bad that I had to carry him out of the tent at night to go to the bathroom.

We took the hound with us when we left, stopping at Ray Cole's Lodge. We told them about the hound. They said, "Oh, the people who lost that dog have been looking for it for ten days." That party had been hunting in Blind Bay before we got there. We left the hound at Ray Cole's Lodge so they could reunite him with his owner, who was from Finland, Ontario.

The last moose hunt on White Otter Lake was not only fruitful, but also rewarding in that we saved that dog's life.

We never went moose hunting after that as the Canadian government raised the price of moose licenses and imposed expensive regulations, such as mandating the use of Canadian guides and Canadian lodges and outfitters. By the time we added up all of the related moose hunting costs, it was less costly to purchase a side of beef.

The Deer Hunt That Became
a Bear Hunt—1975

Clem Hendrickson from Minneapolis, Minnesota; Doc Dobbs from Duluth, Minnesota; and his father, Ernie Dobbs, from International Falls, Minnesota, went deer hunting up on Namakan Lake with my uncle Allen, who was guiding us in November of 1975. Allen had a couple of dogs he was using to hunt the deer. Dogs were permitted for use when hunting in Canada. I can still remember seeing the dogs and the bear nose to nose smelling each other. At that time you could purchase a Canadian license for a hundred dollars, which allowed you to take one deer, one moose, one bear and one timber wolf. Due to the regulations, a Canadian guide was required. Since uncle Allen was a Canadian guide, he qualified.

On Namakan Lake, east of Kielczewski Island and west of Blackstone Island, is Six Deer Island. We took two boats up to drive deer on Six Deer Island. Uncle Allen put Doc Dobbs and his dad, Ernie Dobbs, off the end of another little island very near Blackstone Island and across from Six Deer Island so they could see the deer coming off of Six Deer Island. Clem, Allen, and I were going to make the drive for the deer on Six Deer Island.

When we went to make the drive on foot, Allen was off to my left.

Allen said, "I know there are a doe and a fawn on this island."

I heard a roar, and I said, "Allen, that was a big bear."

Allen said, "No, that was a wolf."

I said, "No, I have heard bear before, and I think I heard him snapping his jaws."

As we were walking the island, we went past the bay. I looked out on the ice and saw what looked like bear tracks in the snow. However, there was only a skiff of snow, just a dusting, so it was hard to tell.

We made the drive and didn't get anything, so we got in the boat and went around to pick up Doc Dobbs and his dad. As we left the island, Allen looked back and said, "Look at that moose up there!"

I said, "No, that isn't a moose! That is a bear!"

In the boat we went around to a narrow section of Six Deer Island. We stopped the boat, and I got out, along with Clem Hendrickson. I told Clem, "If you want to get a bear, stay here." But instead, Clem walked straight east. I told Allen to make sure and put a clip in his gun. His response was, "Ah, a bear won't bother yah."

I stayed in the narrow neck of the island because I knew the bear would come through that way if Allen didn't kill him. Allen took the boat and went around to the end of the island, stopped the boat, and got out. He headed up the hill but did not have the clip in his gun. He stepped over a log. The bear was hiding behind a tree covered in leaves and snow, so Allen did not see him.

The next thing Allen knew, the bear charged out from behind the tree, straight for him. The only thing that saved Allen from the charging bear was his two dogs, which had come through the point following his boat. The dogs jumped in and chased the bear back, away from Allen. The bear ran off with the dogs chasing him. The bear was coming toward Clem, who shot at him.

Allen yelled to Clem, "What way is he going?!"

Clem shouted, "East!"

Allen started swearing because east was Allen's direction, so the bear was coming back to him. Clem shot at him again.

Allen heard the second shot and shouted, "What way is he coming?!"

This time Clem shouted, "West!"

Allen shouted back, "Good!"

The bear was heading west, but he turned and ran out on the ice, likely sensing that I was on the narrow neck of the island. I am not sure how he knew I was there, but he knew, which is why he went onto the ice. The dogs were still chasing him. I took aim and missed him. The dogs were fighting with him at the same time. He turned and went back up into the woods. As he ran back into the woods, he ran past me. As he was going around, I thought, '*I won't aim for your head; I might miss you. I will aim for your heart.*' So I took aim and shot him right behind the right front shoulder. He was forty yards away when I pulled the trigger.

He turned on a dime and charged me straight on with his jaws wide open. He covered those forty yards in less time than it took to snap your fingers. All I could think to do was to keep shooting. I was shooting a 38-55 Winchester lever action on a Marlin barrel with 255-grain bullet. One bullet hit him between the shoulder blades and one in the chest, and with his jaws still snapping he fell only nine feet from me. He knew exactly where I was before I shot him the first time because he was avoiding me, but after the first shot through the heart, he let out a big roar, wheeled, and charged me. He was snapping his jaws the whole time.

When I dressed him out, I saw that his heart was split in four pieces. There were just shreds holding it together. I had missed with the first shot because the dogs were so close that I overshot trying to miss the dogs. The second shot had hit him in the heart from the side, cutting his heart in half sideways, and the third shot hit his heart again from the front, which is why it was split in four pieces. The fourth shot him in his shoulder.

It taught me a lesson: even if you shoot a bear in the heart, when a bear is charging, you can still be killed by it. When the dogs came up, he was doing the death moan and still snapping his jaws. He weighed about 250 pounds.

Allen said that the old lever action sounded like an automatic. When he heard the three shots in quick succession, he knew there would be a dead bear.

He was a beautiful bear. The hair on his hide was two and a half to three inches long. At the end of a long summer of plenty, he had already denned up. His hide was gorgeous. He had been shot previously but was healing. Clem had shot at the bear but missed. If he had stayed on the peninsula, he would have killed him. Keith Thomas wanted the bear, and Clem was supposed to shoot a bear for him. So I gave the bear hide to Keith Thomas, who made a rug out of it.

We did go on to get two deer, a doe and a fork-horned buck, but we did not get them off Six Deer Island.

Chasing a Bear with an Axe is not very Effective—1976

After the S.E.P. camp closed at the end of the summer, we usually went up to Voyageur's National Park as a family to camp. We usually camped on an island called My Island, which is next to an island called Your Island. In late August of 1976, we were all camped on My Island. We had all of the kids and Mardell's mother, Janette, with us. Campers had been feeding a bear, so he was used to taking food from humans. I was sleeping in the tent with the food, and the cotton picker tried to get underneath the tent and at the food that I had laid my head on. All we had was the axe because, again, it was the national park, so no guns were allowed. I chased that bear around in the dark with the axe while Mardell ran around banging on pots and pans and hollering, but we didn't do much other than chase him away for thirty minutes or so. All night long he kept coming back, and we would get up and chase him around in the dark to no avail. Thirty minutes later, he would be back. We wished we had a gun right about then.

Predator Control—1978 to Present

I was contracted to manage the taking of predators for the State of Minnesota and for the federal government as well. I had to take care of some coyotes. I think there was some bear involved in it too. I wound up catching two bear, two deer, four coyotes, one timber wolf, and the owner's dog. The one timber wolf I got was taken by the state and given to the feds, since they were protected at the time.

I had also caught the owner's dog, which I felt real bad about. She didn't, but I did. I was really upset. I also got two deer, one of which I let go. The one I was able to let go had two fawns in her. The other one was a buck fawn. When I talked to Tom, the state game warden at the time, he told me not to feel bad because "it was a killing proposition." The owner had already lost one cow to predators, and another one was walking around wounded with thirty pounds of flesh torn out of her back. I couldn't believe the sight.

The person I had to do this for was a farmer in Orr. She had cattle. It was a hideous sight. There was a cow still alive, and yet she had about thirty pounds of meat chewed out of the back ham. I didn't know whether coyotes, bear, or wolves were responsible, but I thought it was a bear because the cow had long claw marks that looked like bear claw marks on her back.

The state game warden received a letter from the federal government stating that this was a killing proposition. I already had the necessary predator control papers to do this type of work.

We tried to let one bear go, but we ended up killing him. He was caught on a long number nine wolf snare between one front leg and the other, so he wasn't getting choked down. Faster than you could clap your hands, he was several feet up a tree. It worried me when I saw how fast he moved.

The bear came back down the tree. One of my sons-in-law, JR, was with me. We broke off a big snag from a tree and conked him on the head and on the nose. Then JR hit him on the jaw, and I said, "Oh, don't do that," because I didn't want to kill him, just stun him.

While I removed the snare, JR kept the rifle leveled on him in case he came to. That 150-pound bear would have lived once I removed the snare, but unfortunately when JR hit him on the jaw, his head had turned downward, so he ended up choking on his own blood. When I told the game warden, he said he was glad we felt sorry for him, but he was also glad that we got rid of him.

Even though I didn't think that bear had caused too much of a problem, he had. He was one of the bears chewing on the cow. Once we killed the bear, the trouble stopped.

I got around in a truck going down paved and unpaved county roads. I'd park the truck and check things out by walking through the woods and looking for "sign." Once I found that, then I would decide whether to hunt and shoot or trap. The distance I traveled for predator control depended on where the government sent me. I could drive as far as three hundred miles in one day on one assignment.

We did catch another great big bear in one of the same snares. She was a huge female. She didn't have any cubs with her, but she was the largest female bear I ever saw in my life. I'd say she was about pretty near four hundred pounds. One of my other sons-in-law, Glenn, was with me when we caught her.

I caught one deer, which was full of fawns. It was March and she would have delivered in May. Based on her size, I thought she had two fawns in her. I managed to let her go, but I broke my thumb doing so because she kicked me while I was trying to get her out of the snare.

In September of 1992, while I was doing a job for the feds with JR, there was a bear making so much noise that it sounded like two of them. We heard him but didn't know where he was because the leaves in the tree hid him from view. He was sitting up in a tree eating acorns when he fell out of it, crashing to the ground.

We were about forty feet away checking snares and traps, and when he hit the ground, he scared both of us. Thankfully before we could react, he took off on a dead run in the opposite direction.

The Vermilion River Bear—1979

It was around 9:00 p.m., in early September of 1979, after summer camp had closed, when I heard an awful ruckus outside. I went outside, and I saw the dog had treed a bear. The bear was growling and snapping its jaws. I went in and got the .35 Remington Pump Gamemaster with two-hundred grain bullets and shot the bear with one shot right behind the right front shoulder. The bear fell out of the tree, breaking one leg. The bullet had gone through his right front shoulder and lodged in the left front shoulder. When the bear hit the ground, he sprang right up in the air and began running on his three good legs after the dog.

At the same time, my wife was talking to my boss in Pasadena, California, on the telephone. He heard the shooting, and asked "What's going on?!"

My wife handed the telephone to my second-oldest daughter, Sherry, while she went to help me out.

Sherry answered, "My dad is shooting a bear."

Jim Thornhill said, "Well, this something! I am listening to a bear shootout in northern Minnesota while sitting in California!" He asked Sherry, "How big is the bear?"

Sherry said, "Dad said it is about four hundred pounds, but it is a lot heavier now because he is filling it full of lead." Jim Thornhill started laughing like crazy.

Before the bear took off, he took a swipe at the dog. The dog's back feet went up in front of its front feet as it tried to get out of the way. That bear kept running, but he was in the line of sight with the chalet. I didn't want to take a chance and hit the chalet, so I waited until the bear was past it, and I shot. I missed, and the bullet went whining by and ended up in a tree. I called to my third daughter, Pauline, who came out with a flashlight. She and I followed the bear down to the softball field. The bear attempted to climb a tree but couldn't because I had shot him in the shoulder and he had broken his left leg when he fell out of the tree. He was growling and snapping his jaws.

Pauline held the flashlight while I took another shot. The bear was about forty yards away.

My daughter said, "Boy, dad, I hope that you can shoot straight."

I shot the bear right between the eyes. The bear was huge, at least four hundred pounds. It wasn't bear season, so I needed to dispose of it. I thought I would dump him in the Vermilion River. The bear was so heavy that it took four of us to put him in the back of the truck. We took him all the way down the 203 Road across the 491 Road to Vermilion Falls. I took all the back roads to avoid running into a game warden on the more traveled roads. In order to dump him in the river, we had to squeeze him between the bridge rails. The bear was so huge we had to shove hard to squeeze him through.

My wife wanted to put a hat and tennis shoes on him so that when he floated by the tourists at the Crane Lake Gorge he would have been a sight to see. As amusing as it would have been, I declined, as I was more concerned with the law. Bill Stocker was with me and, I was driving pretty fast out to Vermilion Falls.

He asked me, "Why are you driving so fast?"

I told him, "I don't want a game warden to catch me."

He responded, "No game warden is ever going to catch you!"

The Biggest Bear I Ever Shot—1992

We had been having problems with a big bear coming into camp at night. My wife, Mardell, and her friend, Lee Nelson, had seen it on the railroad tracks when they were out walking down the camp road. She was telling me how big it was, but I wasn't excited about it. I said, "Oh, come on, Mardell, you were just afraid and scared."

She said, "No, no, Floyd. I've never seen a bigger bear." Then she told me she threw rocks at it. I don't think I would have done that. She also yelled at it and called it some unrepeatable names. She had to sound mad to scare it off, so she said something like, "Get your big black sorry ass off this track!"

As it turned to lumber off, it was sideways on the railroad tracks, and its rump hung over the railroad track about a foot and a half on one side, with its front sticking out over three feet on the other side. It had to have been seven feet long.

She said, "It is an awful big bear, Floyd."

The next day a bear came into camp. It was near the back of the kitchen next to the dumpsters. Because it was during the middle of camp, with five hundred people around, I shot the bear. It was about four hundred pounds. I thought this was the same bear that Mardell had seen on the railroad tracks. I showed it to her, and she said, "No, it is just a cub, Floyd. That is not the bear at all." It wasn't as big as the bear she had seen the day before. About that time, she had to leave on an ambulance run. She volunteered for a regional ambulance service for fourteen years. She left the car near the ambulance station in Orr, so I had to go get the car.

I drove the camp truck out to get the car. Across Highway 53, I saw something cross the road near a cabin back off the highway. That family, the Longhenrys, had a dog and a couple of little kids. I saw the animal standing on its hind legs. Initially I thought it was a moose. Then I thought, '*No. That is not a moose. It's too wide. Moose aren't that wide.*' It stood with its shoulders stooped and was a good three and a half to four feet wide. I couldn't believe the size of it. When I got close, I saw that its mouth was partly open and the hair was standing up on its back.

I revved the truck, hit the brakes to make them squeal, and began honking the horn. He acted like he was going to come at me. I couldn't turn around, so I backed the truck up. He dropped down on all fours. He was mad, snapping his jaws and talking to himself. He turned and headed down the road toward the Longhenrys. I believe the bear was upset because the Longhenrys' dog had been chasing him.

I went back to camp and told Mardell about it. "I think I saw your bear, Mardell. He is the biggest bear I have seen in a long, long time. I think he might even be bigger than the bear that broke into the cabin on Frank and I up at Pipe Lake, or at least as big as the one my dad shot up on Moose Camp Creek off of Rainy Lake when I was fourteen years old."

I didn't think much more about it. Another family had bought some property about a half a mile from the camp's front gate. They saw the markings of this bear and asked me to get rid of him. They said, "We are afraid of him. He is marking as high as ten feet up. Right around seven feet, he is biting the tree! No bear is that big or that tall in this country."

Around midnight on September 29, 1992, I heard our Pit Bull growl. I wondered what she was growling at, and then I dozed off. I heard something fall over just outside of the next faculty cabin. I got up and looked out through the screen. The temperature had been warm, but it was much warmer now. It was around eighty degrees. I saw something moving. There was a row of three fifty-gallon drums in front of the next house. They sat almost four feet high off the ground. I could see the back of this thing moving behind the drums, sticking up six or seven inches higher than them. I couldn't believe it when I saw it. I said, "That must be a humongous animal." I saw the head sticking out the other end of the barrels. Each of the barrels was thirty inches wide, and I could still see the rump sticking out about a foot on one end and the head on the other.

I whispered to my wife, "Mardell, there is the biggest bear out here."

She was already asleep, and she drowsily replied, "Well, kill him."

I eased over and took the gun out of the case, and it thumped on the carpet. He heard it through the open window; he wasn't more than thirty or so yards away. He took off with the only bag of garbage on the whole campus, which he had taken out of one of those fifty-gallon drums. I took the gun with six shells in it and went outside.

The bear had gone off to the jungle gym, the play area for the children. It was so dark outside you couldn't see your hand in front of your face. He sat down and proceeded to tear that bag of garbage apart, looking for any food that might be in it. I shined the light but couldn't see him anywhere. I had the gun in my left hand and the light in my right hand. The game warden had already heard complaints about the bear, so we needed to get rid of him. He told me that, he would back me up and that I should get rid of him as long as I didn't poison him. And, he didn't care if I had to use a light to shoot him.

I motioned to Mardell, who was standing in the doorway to let Dynamo (Peggy Sue) go. Our dog Peggy Sue came out like lightning and it wasn't three seconds before she was on top of the bear. Mardell hollered, "She treed him already!"

She had already bitten him two weeks before, which we had realized when we skinned the hide. At that time she bit him in the butt and treed him. I remembered later that she had been barking, and I wondered what in the world she was doing. I thought she might have had a deer cornered. What I realized now was that she had the bear treed and was waiting for me to go and get it. When I didn't come to her rescue, she came home.

I realized then that the reason the bear was afraid of her was because she had bitten and treed him before. In thirty seconds, she had that bear thirty-five feet up a tree. The bear was snapping and growling. I took good aim and asked God to direct that shot. I thought I had hit the bear, but there was no reaction. He didn't even wiggle. So I pumped the gun again and took aim with the .35 Remington Gamemaster. I was shooting two-hundred-grain bullets. Again I was sure that I had hit the bear, but it didn't seem to faze it. The bear was that big and powerful.

What I hadn't noticed was that the bear had stopped snapping his jaws and making all that racket. In the meantime, the dog was running around the tree, waiting for him to come back down. I took a third shot and missed him. He was about forty yards away.

I said, "Oh, you mean I am not hitting you?"

Then I saw his head and neck drop down, and I knew he was hit badly. He was thirty-five to forty feet up the tree when he came out of it. The tree wasn't over ten inches in circumference. Usually, they won't climb a tree that small, but he did, and I don't know how he did it. The rip marks on the tree showed that his hind and front feet had imbedded an inch into that Norway pine. I couldn't believe how powerful his paws were. When he hit the ground, the ground shook because he weighed around six hundred pounds, maybe better, and he wasn't fat. That was why he was out looking for food. He only had an inch and a half of fat on him. He had been denned up, but when the weather warmed up, he came out of the den. He was hungry, not fat enough to den up for the winter, and looking for food.

Just before he hit the ground, my wife came running up behind me, barefoot and in her nightgown. I jumped. I was only wearing my T-shirt and shorts, and I was barefooted. She had brought out some additional shells. About that time, our son-in-law, JR, came out to the rescue as he had heard the shots as well. By that time, the bear was on the ground. Peggy Sue had the bear by the top of the head, and I didn't want her to ruin the cape because my boss, Joe Tkach, had asked me five years before to get him a big bear hide. I had told him I would do the best I could.

The bear was stone dead before he hit the ground as the two shots I fired first cut the main artery along the backbone, hitting him dead center. An animal usually lasts about fifteen seconds after the main artery is cut. I didn't realize how much the blood was pumping out. It was pumping out maybe fifteen, twenty feet around that tree, just squirting out from the first shot. The second one hit six inches above it.

He landed on the ground, and when my wife saw him, she said, "I hope that Mr. Tkach doesn't want this bear."

I told her, "No, I promised it to him. I told him I would do my best." I really didn't want the bear.

I told our state game warden about the situation, and he said he would take care of it for us as the bear was a problem to start with. "That is about the biggest bear I have seen," he said.

I gave the bear hide to Joe Tkach. Joe had it tanned and made a bear rug out of it. When he passed away, the bear rug went to his son. His son didn't have enough room for it, so he gave the rug back to me. This was a blessing because my wife wanted it when she first saw it lying on the ground, and I felt bad having to say no to her. They sent it back to me, and I really appreciated it. It was free. It didn't cost me a penny. It was done up for a bear rug in 1993, and at that time it cost about $650. Today it would cost a lot more, so it is a keepsake. It is eight and a half feet from the nose to the tail and eight and a half feet across the paws, which is a huge animal. I have it to this day.

Oh, and the claw marks were still in that tree when I left camp in 2000.

1992 – Pictured here is the biggest bear Floyd ever shot along with his bear dog, Peggy Sue. This bear was shot at the Y.O.U./S.E.P Camp in Orr, Minnesota.

The Renegade Bear—1993

At the end of each summer, we used to go camping with the family up on Namakan Lake. I was not going to bring a gun because we were camping in Voyageurs National Park, and it is illegal to have a firearm or to kill any of the wildlife. However, there were always bear problems up there, so I brought a gun along. I am not one to travel where there is danger and not have some kind of protection. On the other hand, I am not one to go out and just wildly shoot anything.

This bear's reputation proceeded it, because I had already heard about it before we even went up there. I was concerned, thought better of it, and went back and got the gun. Well, sure enough this animal came into the camp the next morning. Our dog, Sandy, started growling. Then I heard somebody at the neighboring campsite hollering. The bear was eating s'mores cookies right off the picnic table. The family was moored off the beach in a houseboat. The bear took off with the bag of cookies. Our children were sleeping in our Lund tri-hull boat on the beach. I grabbed my trusty .35 Remington Gamemaster and took off around the corner of the tent. I ran after the bear and came to the middle campsite on My Island. Sure enough, the bear had chased a lady from that campsite out into the water. She was holding her baby up in the air above the water. Well, at that time, I realized that the bear deserved to die.

I got so mad because according to regulation, you are supposed to call the park ranger, who is usually about twenty miles away by water with no cell phone coverage in that area. When an animal gets like that, he deserves to die. People make more of a deal out of killing an animal then they do killing a person sometimes.

In any case, as a result, every other camper tore down their camp and left. We were on the island by ourselves. I knew that bear was going to come back, so I told the girls to stop sleeping in the boat and sleep in the tent across from ours.

When I discussed this situation with my uncle Allen, he said, "What are you going to do with that bear?"

I said, "I am going to take him off and dump him."

He asked, "How big is that bear?"

I responded, "He looks to be about three hundred and fifty pounds."

The bear was a renegade and had eaten up all of the campers' food and tore everything up. When a bear gets like that, he has come to depend on people, which is our fault.

A couple of days later, two guys came and asked if they could camp off the end of the point near where we were camped. The same bear had run them off and eaten all of their food. They were going back to Crane Lake to get more food. They wanted to leave their campsite there because they thought it would be safer next to ours for the two days they would be gone getting more food.

About eleven o'clock at night, I heard a squirrel chirp. The bear was trying to dig the squirrel out of the ground and eat him. He was getting hungry again. Sure enough, just before daylight, he came back to our campsite. I heard the dog growl again. So I slipped my pants on and looked out the plastic tent window. There he was up on the picnic table between our tent and the tent with our children in it. He was pawing through the condiment containers. When he stepped down off the picnic table, he looked like he was headed toward the girls' tent. So before he got there, I took good aim and said '*Right there is your heart.*' I shot him right through the tent window and right through the heart.

He exploded off the picnic table and whipped around it. I flew out of the tent. He ran right by me, and I shot again, hit a white pine tree, and missed him. He let out a death moan because I had shot him in the heart with the first shot.

Since it was illegal to have a firearm or shoot a bear, we covered our tracks by shooting off firecrackers; washing all the brush, trees, and ground that was covered in blood with buckets of water; and rolling the bear up on a tarp we had been using for a windbreak. Then we placed the tarp in our fourteen-foot open Richline boat, and Mardell and I took off with the twenty-five-horsepower motor "looking for driftwood" for a fire. We motored on over to the Canadian side of the lake, and we hauled him back in the woods. I found a large downed tree and dumped him behind it.

The next day a man came up to one of the campsites with his sixteen-year-old daughter, who was dying of cancer. She wanted to go camping. He told me he was really worried about the bear. He camped next to us because he thought that there would be safety in numbers.

When we went to leave, he told me he was worried about the bear coming back. I told him, "You don't have to worry about the bear. I took care of him." I didn't tell him how we took care of him or what we did with him.

When we went over to the Canadian side to visit my uncle Allen, he asked me, "All right, Floyd, what did you do with the bear?" I let him know that we had dumped him back in the woods on the Canadian side. He said, "That's just like you Americans, dumping your garbage on the Canadian side!"

Well, it was just a matter of getting rid of the bear because I did not want it around. I was really disgusted with that bear because he was not an old bear. He had good sharp claws and nice teeth. He could have fended for himself in the woods. In this case, sooner or later somebody would have been hurt. He had already chased a woman and baby out into the water despite the fact that the family dog was chasing him round and round. In fact, the dog was probably what saved the woman and the baby because the water wouldn't have stopped that bear from coming in after her.

Peggy Sue

One of the dogs we had at camp was Peggy Sue. We got her from the Orr Airport manager. All we knew was that she was part Pit Bull. She was just six weeks old and weighed three pounds when we got her. We took her to a vet and asked whether or not the fact that she was part Pit Bull would cause a problem with the thousand or so children we had at camp each summer. The vet told us that any dog can be made mean. It is all in how you train them.

Peggy Sue never bit anyone. She loved both children and adults. She followed Mardell up to the camp laundry and loved to chase squirrels. Peggy Sue loved to run alongside the truck. When she was about five years old, she was running alongside the camp truck and was accidentally run over when the truck turned. Her right eye was severely damaged. The vet tried to save it, but after several weeks, it had to be removed.

On one occasion, she got into a fight with a muskrat under the dock. They were under the water, and she was bitten on her blind side on the shoulder. The camp doctor stitched her up.

Shortly after that, we had a mean bear down at the wastewater pond. I saw where it had been walking and feeding on the jewelweed that grew alongside the pond. I didn't realize the bear was so close to me. I came to one of the posted signs, which said "Water Table Inspection Hole." The bear had pulled the sign off and chewed it all up for no reason, just dirty-like. I saw a big pile of droppings, and I had no gun. Then I heard a loud snarl. Peggy saw the bear and took after him. She chased him all around the woods. When she came back, the wound she had from the muskrat fight had been torn open again in the fight with the bear. So, the camp doctor sewed her up again.

That bear eventually came into camp. I knew it was only a matter of time before that happened. The security at camp called me about a bear that had come into camp near the Boys Dorm Eight. It was about eleven o'clock at night. I went up there and let Peggy loose. She treed the bear right away. It was dark, and the tree branches were full of leaves. I thought I hit him in the side, but I had actually hit him in the hind foot, and the bullet had traveled up to the front foot. The bear came down the tree and charged after me. The only thing that saved me was Peggy's attacking it. It almost got me because I couldn't get out of the way.

He came straight at me, and Peggy grabbed him by the neck. There was thick maple brush behind me. The bear took a swat at Peggy's blind side and nearly killed her. He cleared her hair off with that swat, and then he took off. I couldn't shoot at him because Peggy was right behind him. I chased him out past the wastewater pond and lost him.

Later on Tom Fink asked me to go down and do a job because the beaver were plugging up Johnson Creek. I heard the same bear moaning. He was cracking in the trees on the edge of the woods, and he kept coming back to camp. He was gun-shy; the minute you pumped the gun, he was gone.

We kept chasing him, and he would run off into the town of Orr. He had a smaller bear that kept him company. Because of his wounded feet, the larger bear would stand on one of his good feet and open the dumpsters, while the little bear would go in and get the garbage. They were both males, but they stuck together. The smaller bear stayed with the larger one because he knew how to get food, and the larger bear stuck with the smaller one because he was able to get food.

One year later to the day after I had first wounded this bear, the camp security called me and said the bear was headed for my house. I stayed up for a while but eventually lay down on the sofa.

Mardell whispered, "Floyd, there is a bear in the yard." The big bear was sitting under our crabapple tree in the backyard. I got up to take a look outside. He heard me move inside of the house. He took off and went around the back of the house, and I went out the living room door and headed him off. There he was bounding away on his two good legs. It was just coming dawn. He was in a direct line of the sailboats, which I didn't want to hit. So I tipped the gun sideways and rolled it back over and hit him a little high in the neck, killing him with one shot. Initially, I thought that I had just stunned him because I hit him high on the neck. I shot him a second time in the neck, but he was dead after the first shot.

Mardell let Peggy out. She whipped out and spun the bear around like a top. She was mad. It was the same bear that had taken a swipe at her and cut her open. He was about 350 pounds. Eventually the little bear that accompanied the male on the dumpster raids came into camp. Peggy chased after him and treed him. I had to shoot him as well. He was about one hundred pounds.

When Peggy Sue was thirteen years old, she developed stomach cancer, and we had to put her down.

Peggy Sue – The One Eyed Bear Dog

Wilderness Survival Skills

I learned a lot of things living where we did. I learned from both my dad and my mother about living in the woods.

One of the main things to remember when you're out in the woods is to keep your cool. Don't panic. Sit down and think it out. Fear kills most people—fear and panic. If you get lost and you have matches, build a big fire. You will get somebody's attention, even if they aren't looking for you.

My dad used to build a fire with his gun. I never did it, but he used to take black powder and build a fire. He used smokeless powder too. I remember him telling me that he was paddling on Rainy Lake one time in a great big high wind. He just barely got to Breezy Island and had no matches. Dad pulled the bullet out and shot the powder into a punky log and then got down and blew on the spark until he had a fire. Black powder builds a fire easily if you just shoot it into a punky log. Punk is found in the middle of rotten logs, and is the part that has not yet rotted. You can get a fire going when you must to survive.

Dad once shot a moose in thirty-five below late in the day. The temperatures were dropping to forty below. He didn't have any matches, so he couldn't build a fire. He skinned the moose and rolled up inside the hide, fur side to him, to keep from freezing. Of course, the ground was frozen around him, but he didn't freeze. I remember him telling me about that when I was a young boy growing up.

In the early days when we traveled, we wore what they called ersatz boots. These boots were made of some sort of synthetic that was much harder than rubber, and it fell apart when exposed to moisture of any kind. The rubber was saved for the war efforts. The Depression made both commodities and work scarce, but the war made it even worse because even if you could scrape together the money, you couldn't buy what you needed since it wasn't available for purchase. We had to make it, grow it, or do without.

Ersatz boots were stiff and had no flexibility. They rubbed my legs raw right through my pants. We usually wore buckskin moccasins with three pairs of socks. You had to be very careful if you ran into slush or fell into a river and got your feet wet. If the water was cold enough to be slushy, it was cold enough to cause frostbite.

Living so far away from towns and other people, my mother and father were very industrious. Mother made her own soap using lard, ashes, and a small amount of lye. Dad made black powder, and smokeless powder, too. Black powder was made by burning birch until the charcoal came off, and then powdering it up real fine. You could make primers. But I wouldn't mess with that. That is a real dangerous situation making up primer ingredients. There are about three ingredients; one of them was mercury. Dad had all of the ingredients to make primers, but I never made them as they were very explosive. The primer he made worked and shot well.

Dad learned a lot about survival from the Indians in the far north near Hudson Bay on the Nelson River. He taught me lessons that I've carried all through my life. It is a matter of knowing how to survive when you live away from others and there's no road or telephone and no way to communicate.

Some basic survival skills my dad taught me that might help you too someday:

✔ Don't look at the bank when you are running rapids; you'll get dizzy and fall overboard. Watch the water.

✔ Eighty percent of your body heat escapes from your head. If it is cold, wearing a hat will make significant contribution to retaining body heat. Because so much heat is escaping from your head, even if a match is soaking wet, if you put it next to your scalp, it will dry out.

✔ Conversely, if you are overheating, pour cold water, if you have it (or any water, if you don't) over your head.

✔ Keep your cool. Don't panic! Fear is what kills most people in the woods.

✔ If you have matches, build a big fire.

✔ If you don't have matches but have gasoline in your outboard motor, you can take the spark plug out, grind it against the metal of the motor so it sparks, and put gasoline on a rag wrapped around a stick. Then touch the rag to the spark, which will ignite.

✔ If you can, carry a magnesium bar, which burns at one thousand degrees Fahrenheit. Shave the magnesium off in a little pile of birch bark, dry grass or dry needles, or small broken-up twigs. Strike the other side of the magnesium bar with the back of a knife or anything you can to make a spark with over the pile of grass and shavings. It will catch on fire right away. As opposed to a lighter, you can drop magnesium into the water, and it won't diminish its ability to build a fire. You can dry the bar off on your shirt and still use it to build a fire.

✔ Always carry a compass, and believe the compass.

✔ Carry three things with you: a compass, a map of the area, and matches or a lighting device, like the magnesium bar.

✔ If caught out in the woods overnight, try to build a fire off of a rock ledge. Put yourself between the fire in front and the rock ledge to your back. In this manner, the fire in front will reflect off the ledge and onto you so that you will have warmth both from the fire on one side and the rock ledge on your backside.

✔ Build a lean-to out of dry, downed wood and pine boughs to keep the rain, wind, and snow off you. When building a lean-to, overlap the pine boughs, placing them downward so that they shed the water.

✔ Cut pine boughs to put on the ground underneath you. The ground leaches heat out of your body, so if you create a layer between you and the ground, you will retain more body heat.

✔ If possible, camp on an island. Bears are more common on the mainland. Also, the winds that blow through an island keep the bugs away.

✔ If possible, camp on an island in an area where the geography makes a natural barrier. It will protect you from strong winds and storms.

✔ Be mindful of camping in low-lying areas, where the bugs will not only be more prevalent but also there is also risk of flooding.

✔ Err on the side of caution. If something looks dangerous, it probably is.

✔ Use good common sense. Common sense is probably your best weapon in the wilderness.

Wesley Spencer (Wes) Kielczewski

Wes was the oldest child of my parents, Orrah and Violet Kielczewski, born on October 31, 1929. Wesley was the only child that was not born at home or delivered by my father. Dad took mother to a nursing home in Fort Frances, Ontario, which is where he was born. Wes's middle name was the family name of my dad's maternal grandparents. The Spencers raised my father and his brother when their mother died in childbirth along with their sister. My grandmother's name was Elnora Spencer Kielczewski.

Wes got a harmonica and learned to play it. Next he got an accordion and learned to play that. It wasn't long before he had a harmonica holder on his accordion and he could play both simultaneously. In the fall of 1952, Wes gave my mother $150, and when she found a piano for sale she bought it. My uncle Paul brought it up and helped get it in the house. It didn't have a bench, so Wes was going to make one. In doing so, he accidentally cut off three of his fingers on his left hand. Later, despite the loss of three fingers, he was still able to play the accordion.

Wes playing the accordion despite his accident.

Wes worked hard, and as he got older, he worked at logging camps. He was very proficient with an axe. He later got into the boat building business out in British Columbia, and when the family moved to Alaska, he moved with them. Wes stayed near and cared for my mother after my father died.

Wes stayed in Fairbanks, Alaska, with the rest of the family and then moved to the Kenai Peninsula, where he leased property on Cohoe Road. He built a forty-five-foot fishing boat named the *Johnny Sue.*

On January 4, 1971, at the age of forty-two, he drowned in the Tustumena River on the Kenai Peninsula when his snowmobile went through the ice. His mitts, boots, and heavy winter jacket were found on the ice nearby, indicating that he taken the heavy wet items off in an effort to get out of the freezing water and onto the thin ice. His body was never retrieved. The local authorities advised that the lake was so deep, cold, and remote that it would be best to not attempt a recovery of the body. It became his watery grave.

Orrah Allen (Orrie) Kielczewski

Orrah Allen Kielczewski, the second child of Orrah and Violet, was born on December 18, 1930. Orrie was also known as Junior. Orrie was born premature and was very small. Our dad did not think he would live very long.

Because of the child's premature birth, Orrah Sr. moved the family seven miles by dog team to Kettle Falls, Minnesota. This allowed the family to be near a store and a doctor in case of emergency.

Orrie was about a year old when he contracted pneumonia. Orrah Sr. sold his old Evinrude motor to buy medication for Junior. They finally obtained the medication, and in a few days, Orrie was better.

He did not walk until he was about three years old. Mom and Dad put him on a harness attached to a clothesline to help teach him to walk.

Orrah Jr. was one of the best under-the-ice trappers who ever lived. In his adult life, Orrah worked as the environmental department head for the State of Alaska's University of Alaska.

Much later in life, Orrah developed Parkinson's disease. After his sister, Elnora, and her husband passed away, he was alone in Alaska. Floyd petitioned the State of Alaska to become his guardian and conservator. Our daughter, Marlette, flew up to Anchorage in March of 2008 and brought him back to Northern Minnesota. He is now in an adult foster care home in Northern

Minnesota. We are happy that we have the opportunity to visit him often.

August 2008 – Floyd and Orrie on La Rue's Island on Namakan Lake, Ontario.

Floyd Everett Kielczewski

Iwas born on December 10, 1932, in the cabin at McKenzie Point, Stokes Bay, which is on the northeast end of Rainy Lake in Ontario, Canada. At the time of my birth, the area was considered an unorganized township of the Rainy River District, and it reads this way on my birth record.

My dad shot a moose that day, and my mother, who was in the early stages of labor, helped to dress it out. A few hours later, at 3:00 a.m., my father delivered me. I was their third child and third son.

The cabin I was born in on McKenzie Point was a log cabin made of rough-hewn white poplar trees built by my father and mother. Moss and mud were used to pack the spaces between the logs. My mom told me that it was the best cabin dad ever built because he took his time and built it right.

Elnora Margaret Kielczewski Moe

We were living at Halverson's Logging Camps when on April 28, 1935; Dad delivered his fourth child and first girl. Dad named her Elnora after his mother and Margaret after her maternal grandmother.

As Elnora grew up, she wanted to go to town more. Eventually Elnora went to Fort Frances and worked in the hospital laundry department. Dad always gave Elnora the position of being in charge of the younger siblings, and she used her authority. Most of the children were not happy as she both a taskmaster and a tattletale. They were happy when she went to Fort Frances. Elnora moved to Ketchikan, Alaska, with the family but then went to Manitoba for several months. When the family moved to Fairbanks, she returned and moved along with them. Eventually they settled in Seward, Alaska. By this time, Frank and Tony had passed away. In Seward, Elnora, at thirty-six years old, married Kenny Moe. They had one son, Benjamin. They lived there for many years.

Before she died, Elnora wrote my mother's biography. It was titled *A Mother's Survival in an Alien Wilderness.* Carlton Press out of New York published it. The book is no longer in print.

In 2003, at the age of seventy, Elnora died of cancer, and two months later, Kenny died of a heart attack at seventy-eight.

Elnora and her husband, Ken, are buried in Seward, Alaska.

Frank Paul Kielczewski III

Frank was born on September 9, 1936. He was named after our paternal grandfather. Frank moved out to Prince Rupert, British Columbia, with the rest of the family in 1956. However, he missed me. So he took the train across Canada back to Mine Centre. Marlette was only six months old, so he figured there would be baby clothes hanging out on the line. When he arrived in Mine Centre, he walked through the town looking for baby clothes on the clotheslines. We were so surprised when he knocked on our door!

Frank joined me guiding on Namakan Lake that summer of 1959. In the fall Frank and I purchased a new trap line, which was located up on the Upper Manitou's Straw and Harris lakes. We bought a trap line that far north because there was nothing available closer to our original trapping grounds. Frank, Mardell, our dog, King, and I went up first to check out the cabins. Afterward, Mardell's parents brought Marlette up to Straw Lake. We made a home out of that lake cabin. By that time, Mardell was expecting what would be our second daughter, Sherry.

In early May of 1960, we flew out in my uncle Allen's seaplane with Mardell and Marlette. We left Frank and the dog up at Straw Lake. Frank seemed to have no fear of the water, often taking chances that I warned against.

Frank wasn't afraid of anything. I remember one time, he had wounded a deer. It was dark out; in fact, it was moonlight. We were tracking the deer in the moonlight. Across the lake, there appeared to be a line of timber wolves on the ice. Frank turned to me and said, "Let's rush them!" I said, "What?! Are you kidding?" He said, "No. I'm not kidding!" I retorted, "Rush them, my foot!" As we walked closer, it became evident that the timber wolves were actually a rock pile. This sort of fearless behavior was typical of Frank.

Dolly Bruce, the owner and operator of Boulder Lodge, had an outpost on Harris Lake. Harris Lake is east and north of Fort Frances and is within thirty miles of the cabin on Straw Lake. Each spring her docks would be flooded from the beaver damming on the lake. She secured a nuisance beaver permit for Frank to trap the beaver after the trapping season had closed. Frank decided to stay up at the trapping cabin for another ten days after we left.

I went back to Mine Centre with Mardell and Marlette to prepare for the summer guiding season that Frank and I would be embarking upon when he finished trapping the beaver. I left my Border collie, King, with Frank. Frank stood out on the ice, waving good-bye as the plane took us out.

On May 10, 1960, Clare Biddeson from Happy Landing Lodge called me to say that King had shown up at the resort without Frank. The Biddesons went up the river to the Straw Lake cabin, but Frank was not there. They feared that Frank was sick.

The dog, King, had to swim three lakes and travel overland a distance of thirty miles to get to Happy Landing Lodge, a familiar area to the dog, which he visited often during the winter months. When King arrived at the lodge, he kept going back and forth to the shoreline of the lake and barking and barking. It was then that the Biddesons realized that something had happened to Frank.

Once I got the phone call from them, I planned to take the train to Fort Frances, where I could get Rusty Myers's Flying Service to fly me up to Straw Lake. I missed the train, which was the first and only time in my life that happened. As a result, I called my uncle Allen on Rat River to come with his airplane and fly me up to get Frank.

When the plane crested the timber line on Harris Lake, the sight of the overturned canoe in the water and the open cabin door stunned both of us. As Allen was landing the plane on the water, Frank's body was visible about eight feet from the shore in ten feet of water. Frank Paul Kielczewski III was twenty-three years old when he drowned in the icy waters on Harris Lake.

Allen and I flew back to Fort Frances and reported the accident to the Ontario Provincial Police. They flew up to Harris Lake with a Royal Canadian Mounted Police officer, recovered Frank's body, and brought it to Fort Frances. We buried Frank in the Kielczewski family plot in Fort Frances.

Evidently, Frank had gone out to fish using a net in the canoe powered by a small outboard motor. The net must have become tangled in the motor, and in an effort to untangle it, Frank got into the icy waters and turned the canoe over completely three times trying to untangle it, and then with hyperthermia setting in, he must have attempted to swim for shore. Even though he was extremely physically fit and youthful, the icy waters got the best of him, and he drowned in only ten feet of water sixty yards from shore. Had he unscrewed the motor and let it drop to the bottom, he would have lost the motor, but not his life.

It was a tremendously difficult time for me. I had lost a good man, my best friend and brother. I sold the trap line in the Harris Lake country and bought another one near where we were living in Mine Centre. Time eases the pain, but Frank's memory remains strong.

Frank is buried in the Fort Frances, Ontario, cemetery in the Kielczewski plot, between his grandfather, Frank Kielczewski I, and his step-grandmother, "K."

Frank on Digby Island off the coast of British Columbia during the period of time he worked at Wahl's boat yard.

Violet Mary Kielczewski Wahl

Violet Mary Kielczewski was born on July 9, 1938. She was named Violet Mary as she was born on our mother, Violet's, twenty-seventh birthday. Young Violet was always helping mother. She would get up early and fix breakfast. She would cut wood for the cook stove using a Swede saw. It never failed that no matter how late I got home, Violet would have a plate of food waiting for me in the warming oven.

When the family moved to Prince Rupert, British Columbia, Violet met Roald Wahl. Roald's father owned a boat building business, where both dad and I worked.

Violet eventually married Roald, but the Kielczewski family would not attend the wedding because they did not approve of Roald. They seemed to have forgotten that mom and dad eloped because mom's parents would not sanction their marriage.

Violet and Roald had two children, Olaf and Kathy. Olaf was born with a fatal disabling disease and was not predicted to live past twelve years old. He passed away at twenty-seven years old. Kathy married and has seven children.

Violet and Roald live in Sechelt, British Columbia. We flew up to Seattle in 2002, drove up to Horseshoe Bay, and took the ferry to Sechelt to visit them. Linda, our youngest sister, and her husband, Lonnie, drove up from Seattle. We all spent the weekend at Violet and Roald's place. I had not seen Violet since 1986, and Mardell had not seen her since 1961. They have a nice home and a beautiful yard. Violet continues to plant a huge garden every year and still cans vegetables. I was happy to see how well they had done for themselves.

Antoine David (Tony) Kielczewski

Antoine David Kielczewski was born on a cold winter day. January 6, 1942, was forty below zero standing temperature with a wind blowing. Tony was named after my dad's great-uncle, Antoine Kielczewski. Tony was a very quiet person who was extremely mechanically gifted. He was always exploring ideas he read in books. Tony got his schooling through the Canadian Correspondence Course. When they moved to Alaska, Tony got a job cleaning at Ellis Airlines. The mechanics there had been working on a Cessna and couldn't figure out where the trouble was. After a few days, Tony told them he knew what was wrong. Mr. Ellis told Tony to go ahead and fix it if he could. He did fix it, and Mr. Ellis told him to hang up his broom.

Tony later got his pilot's license and went to Dallas and got his helicopter license. He flew what was referred to as the "Flying Boxcar" for the Alaskan Pipeline. He stayed in Ketchikan when the rest of the family moved to Fairbanks. He began to fly a Cessna 185 from Ketchikan to Hyder on the Alaskan-Canadian border. On January 16, 1969, just after his twenty-seventh birthday, Tony was taking six hundred pounds of food to a village near Hyder. He flew through a seven-thousand-foot mountain range to get to Hyder. Tony always left his route on the recorder in Ketchikan.

Early 1960s – Tony in Ketchikan, Alaska.

On this day, the weather changed into a one-hundred-mile-per-hour wind. Four feet of snow fell. Tony never made it. The State of Alaska sent out the Grumman HU-16 Albatross Search and Rescue aircraft to search for Tony. The US Coast Guard searched for him for over a month. They told me that if anyone could survive, it would be Tony. Additional funds were raised, and private planes searched for him too. Neither the plane nor Tony was ever found.

William John (Bill) Kielczewski

William (Bill) John Kielczewski was the eighth child and last son of Orrah and Elnora. Billy was born on July 14, 1952, at John Kulauski's place on Brule Narrows. My mother and father had gone to Fort Frances, and on the return trip, her water broke. So dad stopped at John Kulauski's, where he delivered Bill. The afterbirth would not come, so dad took mom back to the La Verendrye Hospital in Fort Frances. My dad, Elnora, and I took the S.S. *Clipper* down to bring mother and Billy home.

We were living at the Falls River homestead, where we lived until we left in 1956. When the family left Ontario, Bill was walking. He was nine years old in 1961 when Mardell, our two girls, and I went to visit the family in Ketchikan, Alaska. We took the train from Mine Centre out to Prince Rupert, British Columbia. From there, we flew up to Ketchikan, Alaska, to visit the family. We stayed one month. On the return, we stopped in Prince Rupert, British Columbia, for three days to visit with Violet and Roald.

After dad passed away, mom, Bill, and Linda moved to Tacoma, Washington. When Bill was sixteen years old, he came to live with us in Orr, Minnesota. He finished high school in Orr, went on to college in northern Minnesota, and worked on the canoeing staff at camp during the summer months.

He met his future wife, Audrey Reek, at camp. She was a counselor for Girls Dorm Two. Bill and Audrey had two boys,

Wesley Grant and Weston Cole. Both boys were named after our older brother, Wes.

Because Bill had never been inoculated, he contracted polio when his infant son, Cole, was inoculated with a live polio vaccine. The drugs used to combat the polio eventually caused pancreatic cancer. After Bill was struck with polio, but before he contracted cancer, he and Audrey had a daughter, Adar. Bill died of pancreatic cancer at thirty-five years old on September 22, 1987. He is buried in Duluth, Minnesota.

Linda Marie Kielczewski Kelly

Linda Marie Kielczewski was the last child and third daughter of Orrah and Violet. She was born on October 25, 1956. When my mother was in labor, I went to get a nurse who lived on Digby Island. The nurse could not get the afterbirth out. So dad, Wes, and I got a canoe, put mom and the baby in it, and paddled across the bay to the wharf. We pulled the canoe up onto the boat and took the boat to the Prince Rupert Harbor. The ambulance came down to the harbor and met us.

After dad died, Linda, Bill, and mom moved to Seattle. Linda married Lonnie Kelly and lives in the Seattle area. They have one adopted daughter, who has six children. Linda worked for Weyerhaeuser for thirty years until her retirement. Linda and Lonnie now live on an island in the Puget Sound. Since she is only a few hours from our sister, Violet, they are able to visit occasionally. Linda and Lonnie spend some part of the winter months in Arizona so we are able to visit with each other when Mardell and I are there.

Epilogue

Floyd retired as the site manager of the Y.O.U (S.E.P.) Camp in Northern Minnesota in May of 2000. He lives with his wife, Mardell, on a farm in Northern Minnesota owned by his daughter, Sherry, and her husband, Glenn Erickson. Floyd and Mardell spend some part of the winter months in Arizona with their daughter, Marlette. They have three additional married daughters, Pauline (JR) Landgren, Sarah (Todd) Schreiber, and Esther (Greg) Landgren, all of whom live in Minnesota. In addition to their five daughters, they have six grandsons, four granddaughters, and two great-grandsons.

Floyd was able to bring his only living brother, Orrah Jr., back from Anchorage, Alaska, in March of 2008. Orrah Jr. currently resides in an adult foster care home near Floyd and Mardell's home. The two remaining brothers derive tremendous joy from spending time together.

Floyd and Mardell have access to a cabin and an island on Namakan Lake and spend as much time as possible up there during the summer months. Floyd still runs the white water of Hay and Lady Rapids and fishes Namakan Lake and River. He still traps nuisance beaver as a bounty hunter for the federal government, and he continues to hunt deer in the fall. In his eighties, Floyd is still an expert marksman and is most in his element in the woods and on the lakes and rivers. In his lifetime Floyd has killed 238 deer, 65 moose, and 68 bears. He truly is a son of the wilderness.

June 2000 – Floyd and his family at his Retirement Party following his retirement from the Y.O.U./S.E.P. Camp in Orr, Minnesota.

2007 - Floyd and Mardell in Hawaii celebrating their 50th Anniversary.

Epilogue

2013 – Current day photo of Floyd on Namakan Lake, Ontario, Canada.

29990665R00181

Made in the USA
Charleston, SC
31 May 2014